Curing the Future

— Current Topics of Health —

健康を科学する

椋平　淳
深山晶子
川越栄子
玉巻欣子
早瀬淳一
福田慎司

音声ファイルのダウンロード/ストリーミング

CDマーク表示がある箇所は、音声を弊社HPより無料でダウンロード/ストリーミングすることができます。トップページのバナーをクリックし、書籍検索してください。書籍詳細ページに音声ダウンロードアイコンがございますのでそちらから自習用音声としてご活用ください。

https://www.seibido.co.jp

Curing the Future
— Current Topics of Health —

Copyright © 2002
All rights reserved for Japan.
No parts of this book may be reproduced in any form
without permission from Seibido Co., Ltd.

はじめに

　現代社会において、「健康」は重要なキーワードの1つになっています。先端医療技術から東洋医学の再評価、肉体面の健康からメンタルヘルス、あるいは"治す"医学から"予防する"医学まで、「健康」に関するニュースがメディアで流れない日はありません。そうした情報を背景として、私たち現代人の「健康」への欲求も、止まるところなく高まっています。

　このテキストは、そうした「健康」関連のトピックについて実践的な英語読解力を養成するために、新聞や雑誌（オンライン版を含む）に掲載された医療・健康・科学関連のホットな話題を選りすぐって編集したものです。

　本書がターゲットとする読解力は、自分の持っている背景知識を最大限に活用して、辞書に頼ることなく、類推力を働かせながら重要な情報を素早く読み取る力です。したがって、本書の Reading にはいわゆる脚注は付いていません。その代わりに、Reading に先行する Orientation や Listening の中で、読解に必要な最低限の背景知識やキーワードが提供されています。同時に、Reading の理解を問う設問は、英文理解のヒントになるように、選択肢の中に重要語句を取り込みながら作成されています。

　また、Listening や Grammar、Vocabulary のセクションでは、各種の資格・検定試験にしばしば使用される問題形式が取り入れられているため、TOEIC® テストなどの試験対策としても利用できます。各セクションの詳しい説明は、次ページの「本書の構成と利用法」をご参照下さい。

　本書が皆さんにとって、現代人に必須の実用的英語力の向上と、私たちの「健康」に関わる現代的な諸問題を理解する一助となることを期待します。

　最後になりましたが、本書の企画・編集についてお世話になりました㈱成美堂の菅野英一氏に心より感謝いたします。

2002 年　夏

編著者

本書の構成と利用法

　各 Unit で扱われる「健康」関連のトピックについて、まず冒頭にあるタイトルを基にイメージを膨らませながら、以下のセクションに進んで下さい。

Orientation
　枠内の日本語文は、各 Unit で扱うトピックの背景説明となっています。これを読みながら、このトピックについて何が問題となっているのかを把握してください。枠下の英文は、日本語文の直訳ではありませんが、内容はオーバーラップしていますから、簡単に目を通すだけでおよその意味は理解できるはずです。英文をさっと読みながら、この Unit の前提知識として必要な 5 つのキーワードを探し出し、実際に記入してみましょう。なお、(　　　) の数は、書き出すべき語数と同じです。

Listening
　資格・検定試験で頻繁に用いられる形式のリスニング問題です。4 つの選択肢が CD で流れますから、それを聴いて、写真やイラスト、図表の内容と合うものを選びましょう。この写真やイラストの内容も、Reading へ進むための背景情報を提供しています。

Reading
　新聞・雑誌に掲載された最新の記事が、どの Unit でも 5 つの段落にまとめられています。Orientation や Listening で提供された背景知識に基づいて、辞書を使わずに類推力を働かせながら、できるだけ早く読んでみましょう。目安は、1 つの段落につき 1 分程度です。段落（パラグラフ）を 1 つ読み終わるごとに、右側のページの設問を 1 つ解答して下さい。選択肢の文面には英文中のキーワードや難易度の高い語句が取り込まれていますから、これをヒントにして英文を理解しなおすことも可能です。一般的に、英語の文章はこうしたパラグラフがいくつも連なったものなので、パラグラフ・リーディングのコツを覚えることによって、どんなに長い文章でも論理の流れを的確に押さえながら素早く読みこなす力が身につきます。

Grammar
　Unit のトピックに関わる英文を利用して、文法のチェックを行います。各種の資格試験などでは誤りを指摘するだけのものが主ですが、このセクションでは正答を記入することで、文法知識の確認と定着を図っています。

Vocabulary
　Vocabulary A も資格試験などでよく見られる形式です。その Unit で学習した知識を活用して、文脈に合う適切な語を選んで下さい。Vocabulary B は、それぞれの Unit の総まとめです。それまでの各セクションに含まれていたキーワードの中から、今後皆さんが学習する際に再出したり、実践活動の中で応用しやすいと思われる語句が 7 つ選ばれています。日本語に対応する英語を実際にスペルアウトすることによって、"使える" 語彙力としてしっかりと定着させましょう。

　各 Unit の並び方は、比較的容易なものから難易度の高いものへと推移しています。また、複数の Unit に共通するキーワードは、基本的には先行する Unit で扱われています。したがって、本書はできるだけ Unit の順序通りに使用されることをお奨めします。

CONTENTS

Unit 1　空の旅にご用心 1
　　　　Experts say economy class can kill

Unit 2　無添加でおいしく 5
　　　　The added cost of convenience

Unit 3　フェロモンでモテモテ!? 9
　　　　Human pheromones

Unit 4　タバコの怖さを再考する 13
　　　　Do you really know the risks of smoking?

Unit 5　潔癖もほどほどに 17
　　　　Cleanliness obsession unhealthy

Unit 6　コンピュータで今日もお疲れ 21
　　　　Technostress

Unit 7　よく効くハーブの長い歴史 25
　　　　Rediscovering nature's healing powers

Unit 8　それでも肉を食べますか？ 29
　　　　Who needs meat?

Unit 9　さぁ、笑って笑って！ 33
　　　　Laughter prescription for good health

Unit 10　長寿の秘密を教えましょう 37
　　　　Ever-growing life span

Unit 11　"秋バテ"退治法 41
　　　　Keeping regular hours can prevent "akibate"

Unit 12　若い者には負けません 45
　　　　Doctors prescribe antiaging therapy

Unit 13	はた迷惑な客 —— 電磁波	49
	Towers suffer wave of protest over health risks	
Unit 14	副作用が知りたい！	53
	Warnings about drugs go unheeded	
Unit 15	世界初のヒトクローン胚	57
	First cloned human embryo	
Unit 16	視力低下にご注意！	61
	Now you see it, now you don't	
Unit 17	患者を護る——人工心臓移植と代弁人	65
	Mechanical heart recipient paired with advocate	
Unit 18	献血したことありますか？	69
	Blood supply could dry up	
Unit 19	今、産むべきか産まざるべきか	73
	Should you have your baby now?	
Unit 20	進化の果ては？	77
	Evolution: Who's responsible?	

Unit 1 空の旅にご用心

Orientation

枠内の下線部 1 ～ 5 は英語で何というでしょうか。下記の英文を参考にして、対応する語句を書き出しましょう。

> 長時間飛行機に乗った後、呼吸困難などの体の不調を訴える人が増えています。これは、長期間 1 窮屈な座席に座っていたために、2 血管中に 3 血の塊ができてしまったことが原因ではないかと言う人もいます。特に窮屈な座席に座らなければならない 4 乗客に起こりやすい傾向があることから、「エコノミークラス 5 症候群」と呼ばれ、時には死に至ることもあります。

A growing number of passengers suffer from the syndrome, in which a clot of blood develops in the blood vessels of their legs after sitting in an aircraft seat — particularly in a cramped economy class seat — for many hours.

1. 窮屈な（　　　　　　　　　）　　4. 乗客（　　　　　　　　　）

2. 血管（　　　　　）（　　　　　）　5. 症候群（　　　　　　　　）

3. 血の塊（　　　　）（　　　　）（　　　　）

Listening 02

CD を聴いて、写真の説明として適切なものを a ～ d から選びましょう。

(PANA通信社)

a.　　b.　　c.　　d.

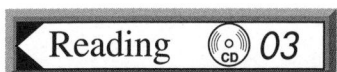

Experts say economy class can kill

Doctors and airlines are urging economy class passengers to take precautions against the so-called "economy class syndrome," which occasionally can be fatal. Victims of the syndrome have died when a thrombus — a clot of blood formed inside a blood vessel — moves, in the normal process of blood circulation, from a vein in the leg and ends up clogging their lungs. The causal relationship between sitting on an aircraft seat for many hours and the syndrome has yet to be proven.

Nevertheless, doctors recommend that those who take long-distance flights exercise their legs, drink a certain amount of water, refrain from consuming too much alcohol and wear relatively loose clothes to prevent blood clots from forming. They also urge passengers to immediately go to a hospital upon arrival if they feel pain in their legs after a long flight.

A clinic at Narita Airport treats at least 100 people a year for what is suspected to be the syndrome. "Those who suffer from the syndrome typically complain that they feel an oppressive feeling in their chest four to five minutes after getting off an aircraft and start walking. We treat 100 to 150 such people a year, including those with only mild symptoms," Toshiro Makino, head of the New Tokyo International Airport Clinic, said.

Makino analyzed the causes behind the 46 deaths that have occurred at the clinic since December 1992. Of them, Makino suspects that 25 are related to economy class syndrome. All of them showed similar symptoms such as difficulties in breathing and decline in the amount of oxygen in their blood. Their electrocardiograms showed they were not suffering from any heart ailment.

The syndrome is not limited to aircraft passengers. It has been reported that passengers on long-distance buses have also developed symptoms typical of the economy class syndrome. A 54-year-old woman suddenly fell unconscious when she got off a night bus at the Ebina service area in Kanagawa Prefecture after an eight-hour ride from Hiroshima in the autumn of 1995. She regained consciousness a few minutes later but suffered breathing difficulties. She was hospitalized for three weeks after doctors found a thrombus in her lung.

(*Mainichi Daily News*, February 19, 2001)

1 ここで述べられている内容と合わないものを選びましょう。
a. 航空会社がエコノミークラス症候群に対して用心するように呼びかけている。
b. エコノミークラス症候群で死亡するのは肺に血栓ができるのが原因である。
c. 最初に血栓ができるのは足である。
d. 飛行機の座席に長時間座っていることがエコノミークラス症候群の原因であると、すでに証明されている。

2 エコノミークラス症候群の予防として、医者が勧めていないものを選びましょう。
a. 足の運動を心がけること
b. ある程度の水を飲むこと
c. アルコールをたくさん飲んで血液を循環させること
d. ゆったりとした服を着ること

3 新東京国際空港クリニックに運び込まれるエコノミークラス症候群の疑いのある患者について、ここで述べられている内容と合うものを選びましょう。
a. 軽症者を含んでも年間100人を越さない。
b. 飛行機内を歩いている間に気分が悪くなる。
c. 飛行機を降りて数分後、胸に圧迫感を感じる。
d. 飛行機を降りた途端に歩けなくなる。

4 エコノミークラス症候群の典型的な兆候として、ここで述べられている内容と合うものを選びましょう。
a. 呼吸困難になる。
b. 吐く息の酸素濃度が落ちる。
c. 心電図に異常が現れる。
d. 血圧が高くなる。

5 長距離バスから降りた54歳の乗客に起こった出来事を選びましょう。
a. 胸部の痛みを訴えて意識を失った。
b. 直後に数分意識を失った。
c. 呼吸困難を訴えた後、意識を失った。
d. 意識を失ったので、検査のため2、3日入院した。

Grammar

下線部a〜cの中で語法が誤っているものを選び、訂正しましょう。

1. She lost a<u>conscious</u> after b<u>feeling</u> a pain in her chest and c<u>was admitted to</u> a hospital.

    [　] → _____

2. There are many a<u>contributing</u> factors that b<u>makes</u> someone more likely to have the syndrome, but scientists don't know c<u>how</u> important each one is.

    [　] → _____

Vocabulary

A. 下線部に入る適切な語をa〜cから選びましょう。

1. The phenomenon has been called "economy class syndrome" because some people thought the problem was linked to the cramped seating in _____ class sections.
    a. coach   b. business   c. cheap

2. The economy class syndrome accounts for a small percentage of diseases in which lungs get _____ with a thrombus.
    a. injured   b. pains   c. clogged

3. Doctors take _____ to see whether the patients' hearts are working normally.
    a. blood   b. electrocardiograms   c. electricity

B. この Unit のトピックに関わる1〜7の基本語句について、対応する英語を枠内から選んで記入しましょう。

1. 血栓	(　　　　　　)	
2. ふさぐ	(　　　　　　)	
3. 肺	(　　　　　　)	
4. 循環	(　　　　　　)	
5. 因果関係	(　　　　　　)	
6. 心電図	(　　　　　　)	
7. 圧迫感	(　　　　　　)	

circulation
thrombus
oppressive feeling
clog
electrocardiogram
lung
causal relationship

Unit 2　無添加でおいしく

Orientation

枠内の下線部 1 ～ 5 は英語で何というでしょうか。下記の英文を参考にして、対応する語句を書き出しましょう。

> 手軽に利用されるコンビニ弁当の1材料には多くの2食品添加物が含まれています。3防腐剤、酸化防止剤、甘味料、香辛料、4人工着色料などです。これらの添加物の中には、5アレルギーや癌を引き起こすものがあります。このような健康への悪影響を考えて、コンビニチェーンのローソンは、「ナチュラルローソン」と名づけた店で添加物の少ない食品を扱う試みを始めました。

　　At Natural Lawson, the shelves are lined with *bento* and *onigiri* rice balls which contain fewer additives. The ingredients of typical *bento* sold at other stores often contain many additives such as preservatives, antioxidants, sweetener, spices, artificial coloring and others, which may cause allergies or cancer.

1. 材料（　　　　　　　　　）
2. 食品添加物（　　　　　　　　　）
3. 防腐剤（　　　　　　　　　）
4. 人工着色料（　　　　　　）（　　　　　　）
5. アレルギー（　　　　　　　　　）

Listening　04

CD を聴いて、写真の説明として適切なものを a ～ d から選びましょう。

(MAMI MARUKO PHOTO)

a.　　b.　　c.　　d.

The added cost of convenience

Take a minute before you join the increasing number of people turning to fast-food items like *konbini bento* and read the label on the packaging; you may be surprised at just how many additives your meal includes. A quick scan of the ingredients might read something like: flavoring, preservatives, antioxidants, sweetener, spices, artificial coloring and others.

If you rely heavily on *konbini bento* or other processed foods, this should raise some health concerns. Recent reports have suggested that some additives may cause allergies or cancer. Even the plastic trays that *konbini bento* come in are believed to contain hormone-disrupting chemicals.

Convenience store chain Lawson, Inc., opened an experimental store, Natural Lawson, in Jiyugaoka, Tokyo, based on the concept of "eating and living healthily" and, of course, conveniently. At the store, 90 percent of *onigiri* rice balls include brown rice instead of white, and all of the *bentos* have fewer additives than their counterparts sold at other stores.

Junichi Ikeda is the leader of the Natural Lawson project team. He said he came up with the idea because his son suffered from asthma and allergies and he was looking for a practical way to improve his family's diet. "I wanted to offer customers food that they can eat without any worries," Ikeda said, "and that became the concept of the shop."

Still, Lawson will continue selling standard *bento*. You needn't completely avoid cheap, packaged meals, according to Toshiki Matsuura, an associate professor of Mukogawa Women's University. He recommends that consumers do a little research on their own to learn more about which additives are bad for them and in which combinations.

(By Mami Maruko, *The Japan Times*, July 29, 2001)

1 ここで述べられている内容と合うものを選びましょう。
a. コンビニ弁当は材料の表示がない。
b. コンビニ弁当は材料の表示が詳しすぎるので、全体を把握するには充分な時間が必要である。
c. コンビニ弁当に防腐剤や着色料などの食品添加物が含まれていることは、表示を見ればすぐにわかる。
d. コンビニ弁当に調味料・防腐剤は含まれているが、甘味料・人工着色料は使用されていない。

2 コンビニ弁当の害について、ここで述べられている内容と合わないものを選びましょう。
a. コンビニ弁当ばかり食べていると、健康上の問題が出てくることがある。
b. 食品添加物のなかにはアレルギーや癌を引き起こすものがある。
c. コンビニ弁当に含まれるすべての添加物に発ガン性のあることが報告されている。
d. コンビニ弁当のトレイには環境ホルモンが含まれていると考えられている。

3 ナチュラルローソンについて、ここで述べられている内容と合わないものを選びましょう。
a. 東京の自由が丘に試験的にオープンした。
b. 「健康によい食事をし、健やかな生活をすること」が基本的な考え方である。
c. 扱っているおにぎりの90％には玄米を使っている。
d. 食品添加物を一切含まない自然食品だけを扱っている。

4 ナチュラルローソンの誕生エピソードとは関係のないものを選びましょう。
a. プロジェクトチームのリーダーの息子が、ぜんそくとアレルギーで苦しんでいた。
b. プロジェクトチームのリーダーが、息子の病状が良くなる食事を考えていた。
c. プロジェクトチームのリーダーが、家族のダイエットに協力していた。
d. プロジェクトチームのリーダーが、お客さんに安心して食べてもらえる食品を提供したいと考えた。

5 松浦助教授が勧めていることを選びましょう。
a. 安価なコンビニ弁当は食べないようにすること
b. コンビニ弁当は買わないようにすること
c. 添加物の入った食品は完全に避けること
d. 消費者が添加物についてもっと知ること

Grammar

下線部a～cの中で語法が誤っているものを選び、訂正しましょう。

1. The Food Sanitation Law _aare strengthened in 1995 _bto address food safety concerns. The law now covers _cso-called natural additives.

   [   ] → _____

2. Ask _ayourself _bthat it is really important _cthat your ham is pink.

   [   ] → _____

Vocabulary

A. 下線部に入る適切な語をa～cから選びましょう。

1. Additives are basically extras that our bodies don't _____.
   a. need   b. limit   c. lack

2. There is no need to be unnecessarily _____ of food additives.
   a. glad   b. peaceful   c. fearful

3. The important thing is to be fully _____ of what kind of additives are in the food you eat.
   a. ignorant   b. interesting   c. aware

B. このUnitのトピックに関わる1～7の基本語句について、対応する英語を枠内から選んで記入しましょう。

1. ファーストフードの   (   )
2. 調味料   (   )
3. 甘味料   (   )
4. 酸化防止剤   (   )
5. 加工食品   (   )
6. 癌（がん）   (   )
7. 衛生   (   )

> processed food
> cancer
> sweetener
> sanitation
> fast-food
> flavoring
> antioxidant

Unit 3 フェロモンでモテモテ！？

Orientation

枠内の下線部 1 ～ 5 は英語で何というでしょうか。下記の英文を参考にして、対応する語句を書き出しましょう。

> 昆虫の世界では、メスがオスを引きつけるためにフェロモンを出します。私たちも最近、セクシーな女性について「彼女は₁フェロモンを出している」というような言い方をしますが、本当に人間にもフェロモンがあるのでしょうか。ある₂科学者は、₃異性の脳に変化を起こす₄性ホルモンに似た₅化学物質についての報告を行いました。果たしてこれが人間のフェロモンなのでしょうか。

While human pheromones have long been fixed deeply as real in the public imagination, scientists were not convinced. The new research found that certain chemicals similar to the male and female sex hormones trigger distinctive brain activity when sniffed by the opposite gender.

1. フェロモン（　　　　　　　）　4. 性ホルモン（　　　　　）（　　　　　）

2. 科学者　（　　　　　　　）　5. 化学物質（　　　　　　　　）

3. 異性　　（　　　）（　　　）

Listening 06

CD を聴いて、写真の説明として適切なものを a ～ d から選びましょう。

(ロイター・サン)

a.　　b.　　c.　　d.

Human pheromones

Brain scans of two dozen volunteers in Sweden found that a part of the brain involved in regulating sexual behavior lit up when women were exposed to a substance similar to male sex hormone, while the same brain area in men lit up when they were exposed to a substance similar to female sex hormone.

The research, which demonstrated that the effect of these chemicals on the brain is not because of their odor, will be of interest to romantics, pharmaceutical companies and researchers of armpit chemistry.

While human pheromones have long been embedded as real in the public imagination, spawning a great market in perfumes aiming to turn on the opposite sex, scientists were not convinced. The new research suggests that at least some human behavior may be unconsciously influenced by invisible chemicals with no obvious odors.

"It's great, it's very exciting and very interesting," says Noam Sobel, a scientist at the University of California at Berkley. No visual or auditory signal that he could think of, says Sobel, has ever been known to produce so sharp a distinction between men and women. "Is it proof that these are pheromones?" asks Sobel. "No, but it is another block in the wall and it is a block in the wall that closes up the hole."

While animal studies have shown that the part of the brain activated (the hypothalamus) is associated with reflexive sexual responses, it remains unclear whether humans necessarily respond in similarly predictable ways.

(*The Washington Post*, September 6, 2001)

1 ここで述べられている内容と合うものを選びましょう。

a. 女性が女性ホルモンに似た物質に接した時、性行動の統制に関わる脳の部分が働くことが分かった。
b. 男性が男性ホルモンに似た物質に接した時、性行動の統制に関わる脳の部分が働くことが分かった。
c. 女性が男性ホルモンに似た物質に接した時、性行動の統制に関わる脳の部分が働くことが分かった。
d. 男性と女性のどちらのホルモンも、性行動の統制に関わる脳の部分には作用しないことが分かった。

2 この化学物質に関心を持つ者として、ここで言及されていないものを選びましょう。

a. 空想家
b. 製薬会社
c. わきの下の化学の研究者
d. フェロモンの研究者

3 ここで述べられている内容と合うものを選びましょう。

a. 人間のフェロモンを売り買いする市場が存在する。
b. 異性の興味をひくための香水が売れている。
c. 科学者たちはフェロモンの存在をはっきりと認めている。
d. 人間の行動は、はっきりしたにおいはあるが目には見えない化学物質に影響を受けていることが分かっている。

4 Noam Sobel の発言内容と合わないものを選びましょう。

a. この化学物質はとても興味深い。
b. この化学物質ほど男女の間で違いをはっきりさせる信号はこれまでになかった。
c. この化学物質が人間のフェロモンの存在を証明した。
d. この化学物質は人間のフェロモンの解明を一歩進めた。

5 脳の視床下部と性的反射の結びつきについて解明されているものとして、正しいものを選びましょう。

a. 動物における結びつきだけがはっきり分かっている。
b. 人間における結びつきだけがはっきり分かっている。
c. 動物と人間の両方において、はっきりとした結びつきが分かっている。
d. 動物と人間の両方において、はっきりとした結びつきが分かっていない。

Grammar

下線部a〜cの中で語法が誤っているものを選び、訂正しましょう。

1. While the subjects breathed the _achemicals for a minute, the researchers _bconduct scans of their _cbrains.

    [　] → _____

2. _aNo of the chemicals seemed to be _bparticularly striking in _cterms of odor.

    [　] → _____

Vocabulary

A. 下線部に入る適切な語をa〜cから選びましょう。

1. Besides sex, pheromones are widely _____ in regulating other behavior in the animal world.
    a. invested   b. involved   c. interviewed

2. Scientists have been unable to identify any specific _____ that clearly act like pheromones.
    a. responses   b. brains   c. chemicals

3. Researchers _____ a dozen men and a dozen women to different smells, such as plain air, vanilla, etc.
    a. examined   b. exposed   c. exceeded

B. このUnitのトピックに関わる1〜7の基本語句について、対応する英語を枠内から選んで記入しましょう。

1. 物質	(	)
2. におい	(	)
3. 走査	(	)
4. 性的反応	(	)
5. 視床下部	(	)
6. 目に見えない	(	)
7. さらす	(	)

```
scan
invisible
substance
odor
expose
hypothalamus
sexual response
```

Unit 4 タバコの怖さを再考する

Orientation

枠内の下線部 1 ～ 5 は英語で何というでしょうか。下記の英文を参考にして、対応する語句を書き出しましょう。

> 喫煙が1肺がんをはじめ健康に様々な害を及ぼすことは、欧米ではもう常識となっていますが、日本ではまだ2喫煙者の割合が大変多いのが現状です。タバコは、一度吸い始めると3中毒になるため、4やめるのが難しいのです。昨今はまた、タバコが、喫煙者本人だけでなく、その周りにいる人々にも害をおよぼすことが明らかになってきました。5たばこ業界に対する責任の追及も始まっています。

A large number of smokers in Japan deeply regret acquiring the hard-to-quit habit. A patient of lung cancer said smokers are also victims of the tobacco industry. "I started smoking when I was about 13," he said. "Then I simply got addicted and could not quit until I found out it was actually killing me."

1. 肺がん（　　　）（　　　）
2. 喫煙者（　　　　　　）
3. 中毒になる（　　）（　　）
4. やめる（　　　　　　　）
5. たばこ業界（　　　）（　　　）

Listening 08

CDを聴いて、イラストの説明として適切なものをa～dから選びましょう。

a.　b.　c.　d.

(KINKO TAMAMAKI)

Do you really know the risks of smoking?

Due partly to people's ignorance of the health risks, Japan has the fourth-highest smoking rate in the world. According to a survey conducted by Japan Tobacco (JT), 53.5 percent of the adult men and 13.7 percent of the women were smokers as of May.

The Health, Labor and Welfare Ministry acknowledged that smoking increases health risks and that tobacco is highly addictive. In its white paper in 1997, the ministry stated that cigarettes contain more than 4,000 chemical substances, including more than 40 carcinogens, and that smoking increases the risk of death from lung cancer by a factor of 4.5 and significantly increases the risk of other forms of cancer.

The white paper says smoking increases the risk of heart attack 1.7 times, and the possibility of other diseases. It also mentions the serious health risks to pregnant women and fetuses, and the damage caused by secondhand smoking, especially to children. Referring to a report by the World Health Organization, the ministry estimates that around 100,000 Japanese annually die prematurely from tobacco-related diseases.

Responding to the scientific evidence of the risks of smoking, the health ministry has conducted programs to urge minors to stay away from smoking, to promote smoke-free environments and to assist smokers in quitting smoking since 1995. A part of a nation-wide 10-year health plan, 'Health Japan 21,' seeks to raise public awareness of the health risks associated with smoking.

"From the perspective of public health, making the nation's smoking population smaller is a priority, but the public still remains ignorant of many of the risks," said the director of the ministry's lifestyle-related disease control division. "We cannot overlook the cost of smoking to our country, in the forms of premature deaths and of additional medical expenses."

(By Hiroshi Matsubara, *The Japan Times*, August 10, 2001)

1 ここで述べられている内容と合うものを選びましょう。
a. タバコによる健康への害をよく知っているにもかかわらず、日本人の多くが喫煙している。
b. 日本よりも喫煙者の割合が高い国は、4つある。
c. 調査によると、成人男性の約半数が喫煙している。
d. 女性の喫煙者数は、男性の喫煙者数よりも多くなってきている。

2 厚生労働白書の記述について、ここで述べられている内容と合うものを選びましょう。
a. 厚生労働省はタバコの危険性を認めていない。
b. タバコはあまり中毒性がない。
c. タバコには4000種類の発ガン物質が含まれている。
d. 喫煙をすると、肺がんによる死亡の危険性が4.5倍になる。

3 喫煙の害について、ここで述べられている内容と合うものを選びましょう。
a. 喫煙によって危険性が高くなる病気は、心臓発作だけである。
b. 妊婦やその胎児には、あまり危険性はない。
c. 喫煙者の周りで煙を吸う子供たちにも深刻な害が及ぶ。
d. これまでに10万人近い日本人が、タバコが原因で起こる病気で早死している。

4 旧厚生省が行なった禁煙促進計画の内容として、ここで述べられている内容と合わないものを選びましょう。
a. 未成年者にタバコを吸わないよう働きかけている。
b. 自由に喫煙できる環境も増やしていく。
c. 喫煙者が禁煙するのを援助する。
d. 喫煙のもたらす健康への害を人々に広く知らせる。

5 ここで述べられている内容と合うものを選びましょう。
a. 公衆衛生の観点から、わが国の喫煙人口を少なくすることが第一である。
b. 喫煙のもたらす危険性について人々の知識は深まった。
c. 厚生労働省の生活習慣病対策室長は、喫煙者は国に対して損害を与えていないと言っている。
d. 喫煙による国民の早死や余分な医療費支出は、国にとって損害であるとは言えない。

Grammar

下線部a~cの中で語法が誤っているものを選び、訂正しましょう。

1. JT has _aclaiming that the health risks associated with _bsmoking have not been scientifically _cproven.

    [　] → ＿＿＿＿＿＿＿＿＿＿

2. About 64.2 percent of smokers want to _aeither quit smoking or reduce _bthe number of cigarettes _che smoke.

    [　] → ＿＿＿＿＿＿＿＿＿＿

Vocabulary

A. 下線部に入る適切な語をa~cから選びましょう。

1. After smoking more than 60 cigarettes a day for more than 30 years, he was hit with a serious ＿＿＿＿＿＿.
    a. smoke   b. program   c. disease

2. The tobacco industry continues selling tobacco to minors by taking advantage of their ＿＿＿＿＿＿ of the health risks.
    a. ignorance   b. importance   c. danger

3. It has been common knowledge in Western countries that tobacco causes ＿＿＿＿＿＿ health risks, of lung cancer for instance.
    a. better   b. worse   c. higher

B. この Unit のトピックに関わる1~7の基本語句について、対応する英語を枠内から選んで記入しましょう。

1. 中毒性の　　　　（　　　　　　）
2. 化学物質　　　　（　　　　　　）
3. 発ガン物質　　　（　　　　　　）
4. 間接喫煙　　　　（　　　　　　）
5. 早死　　　　　　（　　　　　　）
6. 妊婦　　　　　　（　　　　　　）
7. 未成年者　　　　（　　　　　　）

```
chemical substance
minor
carcinogen
pregnant woman
addictive
premature death
secondhand smoking
```

Unit 5 潔癖症もほどほどに

Orientation

枠内の下線部1～5は英語で何というでしょうか。下記の英文を参考にして、対応する語句を書き出しましょう。

> 1消臭製品の人気は根強いものがあるようです。テレビコマーシャルの中には、2顕微鏡で拡大された3細菌や寄生虫などが活発に動き回ったり、4不潔を嫌う登場人物が大きな叫び声を上げたりするものもあります。汚れ5に対して偏執症になる人がますます増えていく私たちの社会の未来は、いったいどうなっていくのでしょうか。

Consumption of deodorizing products is rising as the preference for extreme cleanliness spreads nationwide. Some television commercials for these products use a microscope to show bacteria and parasites while a voice on the soundtrack screams about filth. It is not surprising that many people become obsessed by cleanliness.

1. 消臭製品（　　　）（　　　）　4. 不潔（　　　　　　　）

2. 顕微鏡（　　　）　5. ～に対して偏執症になる（　　）（　　）（　　）

3. 細菌（　　　　　）

Listening 🎧 10

CDを聴いて、写真の説明として適切なものをa～dから選びましょう。

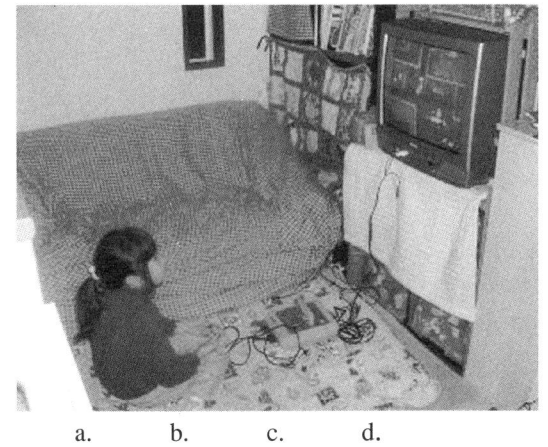

a.　b.　c.　d.

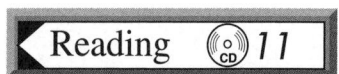

Cleanliness obsession unhealthy

Everyday goods made from bacteria-resistant materials are available including ball-point pens and underwear, as are bacteria-resistant baseball gloves that do not smell bad. A device that automatically places a paper cover over the toilet seat so people do not have to make contact with it is becoming popular.

Japanese people tend to be excessively sensitive to smells, despite having much lighter body smells than some foreigners. The tendency to be abnormally averse to smells is especially noticeable among people in their late teens and early 20s, and in some instances, children.

According to some ethnologists, Japanese people's hatred of *kegare* (impurity) and *yogore* (filthiness) are national characteristics dating back to ancient times. It seems that aversion to smells is embedded in the Japanese culture. The revulsion that today's young people show for their body odor seems almost like disgust with their own bodies.

Prof. Koichiro Fujita of Tokyo Medical and Dental University says, "Today's human body is genetically the same as it was 10,000 years ago." The human body has always had cells to deal with most bacteria and parasites found in nature and to interact with elephants, giraffes and other animals, according to the professor.

"Many people will have fewer opportunities for their cells to use their full capabilities handed down by their ancestors," Fujita said. "I am deeply concerned that the reduced use of the cells' capabilities may cause society to become increasingly fragile." Problems that accompany developments in this direction are likely to increase in this age of information technology.

(*The Daily Yomiuri*, September 7, 2001)

1 ここで取り上げられていない製品を選びましょう。
a. 抗菌仕様のボールペンや下着
b. 抗菌仕様でにおわない野球のグローブ
c. 抗菌仕様でにおわない剣道の防具
d. 便座の上に置く紙シート

2 自分の身体のにおいを異常に嫌う年代として、ここで挙げられているものを選びましょう。
a. 10代後半
b. 20代後半
c. 30代後半
d. 老人

3 民俗学者の学説として、ここで述べられていないものを選びましょう。
a. 日本人が不潔なものを嫌悪する気質は、古代までさかのぼることができる。
b. 日本人が不潔なものを嫌悪する気質は、日本文化の中に内在している。
c. 若者が自分の臭いを嫌悪するのは、自らの身体そのものを嫌悪しているかのようである。
d. 若者が自分の臭いを嫌悪するのは、現実から逃避したいからである。

4 人間が常に維持してきた能力として、ここで述べられているものを選びましょう。
a. 1万年前と同じ体力
b. 細胞レベルで、自然界にあるほとんどの細菌や寄生虫に対処する力
c. どのような自然条件にも順応していく能力
d. 象やキリンなどの動物を打ち負かす能力

5 未来の社会で起こることとして、ここで予想されているものを選びましょう。
a. 人類は、その細胞が持つ能力を子孫に伝えなくなる。
b. 人類は、その細胞が持つ能力を十分に活用するようになる。
c. 人類がその細胞の持つ能力を活用しなければ、社会そのものがもろくなる。
d. IT（情報技術）が問題を解決してくれる。

Grammar

下線部a〜cの中で語法が誤っているものを選び、訂正しましょう。

1. People rarely _ado _binteract with such animals as elephants and giraffes, thus depriving the cells _cfrom their jobs of dealing with various creatures.

    [ ] → _____

2. The more children get nervous _aabout personal cleanliness, _bless they tend to play games _cthat involve touching or tackling each other.

    [ ] → _____

Vocabulary

A. 下線部に入る適切な語をa〜cから選びましょう。

1. The _____ product market now has annual sales of ¥60 billion.
    a. sensitive   b. deodorizing   c. microscopic

2. If others tell you that your clothes are dirty when really there is just a small spot, you may feel _____ about what others think of you.
    a. fine   b. embarrassed   c. popular

3. The extent to which today's young people are so intent on being odorless seems _____.
    a. ancient   b. available   c. excessive

B. このUnitのトピックに関わる1〜7の基本語句について、対応する英語を枠内から選んで記入しましょう。

1. 消臭の   (   )
2. 抗菌の   (   )
3. 神経質な   (   )
4. 潔癖症   (   )
5. 嫌悪   (   )
6. 遺伝的に   (   )
7. 寄生虫   (   )

> genetically
> deodorizing
> parasite
> sensitive
> bacteria-resistant
> disgust
> cleanliness obsession

Unit 6 コンピュータで今日もお疲れ

Orientation

枠内の下線部 1 ～ 5 は英語で何というでしょうか。下記の英文を参考にして、対応する語句を書き出しましょう。

> あなたはコンピュータや携帯電話がない生活に耐えられますか？ ある 1 臨床心理学者が、コンピュータ業務などに従事することによってもたらされるストレスのことを「2 テクノストレス」と名づけました。テクノロジーに対する 3 不安と 4 中毒が 5 症状ですが、コンピュータや携帯電話の爆発的な普及とともに、一般の人たちの間にも広がっています。あなたは大丈夫ですか？

The word "technostress" was coined by clinical psychologist Craig Brod in his 1984 book *Technostress: The Human Cost of the Computer Revolution*. In the book, he identifies the two major symptoms of technostress — techno anxiety and techno addiction. The symptoms first appeared among computer experts, but these days, they are no longer limited to specialists.

1. 臨床心理学者（　　　　　）（　　　　　）　　4. 中毒（　　　　　　　　　）

2. テクノストレス（　　　　　　　　）　　5. 症状（　　　　　　　　　）

3. 不安（　　　　　　　）

Listening 💿12

CD を聴いて、写真の説明として適切なものを a ～ d から選びましょう。

a.　　b.　　c.　　d.

Technostress

"I've been seeing patients with techno anxiety since the bubble economy days, when computers were introduced to Japanese companies," says Toru Sekiya, director of the Hatsudai Clinic. "But the patients I see today suffer from techno addiction more." Techno anxiety usually afflicts middle-aged people who find that their skills have become outdated in the face of new technology — their anxiety often leading to neurosis.

The symptoms of techno addiction first appeared among computer engineers and software programmers. Techno addicts do not think of their addiction as an illness. They isolate themselves from all forms of human interaction. As a result, they may come to suffer from depression.

But what is alarming medical experts today is that techno addiction is no longer limited to specialists. "With the use of cell phones and e-mail spreading, technostress has become a social problem," says Sekiya. "Cell phones have made it possible for the owners to be reached 24 hours a day, leaving them no time to themselves. E-mail may be convenient, but for those who get 100 to 200 messages a day, it's just too much to deal with."

According to the Ministry of Public Management, Home Affairs, Posts and Telecommunications, the number of cell-phone owners increased from 27 million in 1996 to 68 million in 2001. The number of Internet users also rose dramatically, registering a fourfold increase from 11.5 million in 1997 to 47 million in 2001.

"Computers were originally supposed to be a medium to make life easier," Sekiya continues, "but we have become slaves to computers instead. Because computers never need a rest, we cannot keep pace with them. Before we know it, we are in front of the computer day and night without a single conversation with anyone around us."

(By Masami Ito, *The Japan Times*, February 24, 2002)

1 ここで述べられている内容と合わないものを選びましょう。
 a. バブル経済以降、関谷院長はテクノ不安を感じている患者を診察してきた。
 b. 関谷院長は現在、テクノ不安を感じている患者を一番多く診察している。
 c. 自分の技術が時代遅れになったと感じる中年世代の多くがテクノ不安に悩む。
 d. テクノ不安はしばしばノイローゼへと悪化する。

2 テクノ中毒者について、ここで述べられている内容と合うものを選びましょう。
 a. 初めのうちは、中高年層が多かった。
 b. 自分たちが病気であることを自覚している。
 c. 他人との普段の会話は普通に行っている。
 d. うつ病になってしまう人もいる。

3 専門家以外にもテクノストレスが広がっている理由として、ここで述べられていないものを選びましょう。
 a. 携帯電話と電子メールが普及したこと
 b. 携帯電話のせいで、ほっとする時間がもてなくなったこと
 c. 電子メールの普及で、携帯電話をかける時間がなくなったこと
 d. 電子メールで1日100を超えるメッセージを受け取ると対処できないこと

4 総務省の報告として、ここで述べられている内容と合わないものを選びましょう。
 a. 携帯電話の所有者は、1996年は270万人だったが、2001年には680万人になった。
 b. 携帯電話の所有者は、1996年から2001年の間に約2.5倍になった。
 c. インターネットのユーザーは、2001年には4700万人にのぼった。
 d. インターネットのユーザーは、1997年から2001年の間に約4倍になった。

5 ここで述べられている内容と合うものを選びましょう。
 a. コンピュータのおかげで、人間はゆとりある生活を送っている。
 b. 人間はコンピュータの奴隷になっている。
 c. 人間と同様、コンピュータもときどき休息が必要である。
 d. 人間は、他の誰かと話をする時でも、コンピュータを手離せなくなってきている。

Grammar

下線部a～cの中で語法が誤っているものを選び、訂正しましょう。

1. Video terminal workers should take a _a15-minutes _bbreak every _chour.

    [　] → _____

2. We must find a solution to protect ourselves _afrom technostress not by getting rid of computers, but by learning _bhow to coexist with _cit.

    [　] → _____

Vocabulary

A. 下線部に入る適切な語をa～cから選びましょう。

1. He went to the hospital, where he was _____ as having technostress.
    a. addicted   b. become   c. diagnosed

2. Companies are beginning to realize that having _____ and physically healthy employees does benefit them.
    a. poorly   b. mentally   c. seriously

3. Some companies have started installing a warning system on their computers, which _____ a message when a worker has been in front of the terminal for too long.
    a. understands   b. thinks   c. displays

B. この Unit のトピックに関わる１～７の基本語句について、対応する英語を枠内から選んで記入しましょう。

1. うつ病　　　　（　　　　　）
2. ふれあい　　　（　　　　　）
3. 媒体　　　　　（　　　　　）
4. 孤立させる　　（　　　　　）
5. ノイローゼ　　（　　　　　）
6. テクノ中毒　　（　　　　　）
7. 苦しませる　　（　　　　　）

| medium |
| techno addiction |
| interaction |
| neurosis |
| depression |
| isolate |
| afflict |

Unit 7 よく効くハーブの長い歴史

Orientation

枠内の下線部 1 ～ 5 は英語で何というでしょうか。下記の英文を参考にして、対応する語句を書き出しましょう。

> 人類がハーブを使用してきた歴史は紀元前5000年頃の古代メソポタミア時代までさかのぼります。以来、ハーブは洋の東西を問わず、1薬・調味料・香料など様々な用途で使われてきました。日本でも広く愛好されています。最近、病気を2癒す目的で、3エッセンシャルオイルを使用する4アロマセラピーが5皮膚科などで注目されつつあります。自然が育むこの薬の大きな利点は、副作用がないことです。

Herbs have been used as medicine, flavoring or for healing all over the world. Today the holistic practice of medical aromatherapy is a common aid in the field of dermatology, because essential oils used in this therapy do not have side effects.

1. 薬（　　　　　　　　）　4. アロマセラピー（　　　　　　　　　）

2. 癒す（　　　　　　　）　5. 皮膚科（　　　　　　　　　　　　　）

3. エッセンシャルオイル（　　　　　　）（　　　　　　）

Listening 🎧 14

CDを聴いて、写真の説明として適切なものをa～dから選びましょう。

a.　　b.　　c.　　d.

Rediscovering nature's healing powers

Records of their use can be found in the ruins of Mesopotamia, dating back to 5,000 B.C. In the fifth century B.C., the Greek physician Hippocrates documented their various medical benefits, and, later, Roman armies took them into battle to heal the wounded. Through the Roman conquests, and later in the Crusades, they spread through Europe and beyond. What are 'they'? Herbs, of course, nature's healers.

In a broad sense, herbs are any plant used as medicine, seasoning or flavoring. They include thyme and sage, which have antibacterial properties; mint and fennel, which are good for digestion; and chamomile and passionflower, which are believed to relieve tension and irritation. Seasoning herbs include parsley and oregano — to name just a few.

Although Japan has benefited from China's long and rich history of herb use, its fascination with Western herbs is a relatively recent phenomenon. The nation now enjoys a potpourri of Western herbs. You'll find cafés serving fragrant herb teas and esthetic salons using essential oils for aromatherapy. Trendy gift shops sell scented pillows and sachets.

While the recent interest in Western herbs has focused on their relaxation benefits, gradually more attention has been gathering around medical aromatherapy. Originating in Belgium and France, its practice involves applying essential oils directly onto the skin and is a common aid in the fields of dermatology, etc. In hospitals using the approach, essential oils are carefully prescribed to treat specific symptoms.

In Japan, grassroots awareness of herbs is growing. The major benefit of herbs is that they do not have side effects. Of course, we can just buy dermatological ointments and sedatives at the drugstore, but there is something comforting about letting nature heal us. Could it be that we are actually uncovering the secrets of ancient Mesopotamia?

(By Mami Maruko, *The Japan Times*, May 13, 2001)

1 ハーブに関する歴史として、ここで述べられていないものを選びましょう。
 a. 紀元前5000年頃、エジプトでは死後の王位を維持するためにハーブを用いた。
 b. ギリシャの医師ヒポクラテスは、ハーブの様々な治癒力を文書に残している。
 c. ローマの軍隊は、負傷兵の傷を治すために、ハーブを戦場に持って行った。
 d. 十字軍などによって、ハーブはヨーロッパやそれ以外の国々にも広められた。

2 ハーブの効用として、ここで述べられていないものを選びましょう。
 a. タイムやセージが持つ抗菌作用
 b. ミントやウイキョウが持つ消化促進作用
 c. カモミールやパッションフラワーが持つ緊張感などを和らげる作用
 d. パセリやオレガノが持つ整腸作用

3 最近の日本でのハーブの広まりについて、ここで述べられていないものを選びましょう。
 a. 中国から伝わった漢方が急速に流行している。
 b. 喫茶店でハーブティーを出している。
 c. エステティックサロンでエッセンシャルオイルを使っている。
 d. ハーブの枕やハーブの匂い袋が売られている。

4 医療としてのアロマセラピーについて、ここで述べられている内容と合うものを選びましょう。
 a. 世界的に急速に注目されるようになった。
 b. ベルギーやフランスで始まった。
 c. エッセンシャルオイルを使うが、直接皮膚には塗らない。
 d. 病院での治療ではエッセンシャルオイルは処方されない。

5 ハーブの大きな利点として、ここで述べられている内容と合うものを選びましょう。
 a. だれでもよく知っていること
 b. アロマセラピーへの利用が可能であること
 c. 副作用がないこと
 d. 古代メソポタミアの秘術が隠されていること

Grammar

下線部a~cの中で語法が誤っているものを選び、訂正しましょう。

1. She has studied herbs extensively and ₐhad written her own books ᵦon herbs, ᵢincluding *Becoming Healthy with Aromatherapy*.

    [   ] → _____

2. She ₐhas created her own herb combinations that ᵦis effective ᵢin treating her stress.

    [   ] → _____

Vocabulary

A. 下線部に入る適切な語をa~cから選びましょう。

1. Certain herbs have some effects on _____ such as the stomach or the intestines.
    a. skins   b. bones   c. organs

2. She has found that certain herbs can be effective in relaxing her and _____ stress.
    a. relieving   b. refusing   c. increasing

3. The lavender aroma is really _____ and it makes people feel relaxed.
    a. risky   b. healing   c. colorful

B. この Unit のトピックに関わる 1~7 の基本語句について、対応する英語を枠内から選んで記入しましょう。

1. 医師　　　(　　　　　　)
2. 皮膚　　　(　　　　　　)
3. 鎮静剤　　(　　　　　　)
4. 調味料　　(　　　　　　)
5. 芳香　　　(　　　　　　)
6. 治療　　　(　　　　　　)
7. 楽にする　(　　　　　　)

seasoning
physician
relieve
treatment
aroma
sedative
skin

Unit 8 それでも肉を食べますか？

Orientation

枠内の下線部 1 ～ 5 は英語で何というでしょうか。下記の英文を参考にして、対応する語句を書き出しましょう。

> あなたは肉と野菜ではどちらが好きですか。「もちろん肉！」と答えた人は、肉を食べることが₁心臓病や癌の原因になることを知っていましたか。一方、₂ベジタリアンの日常の食事は、脂肪やコレステロールが少なく繊維が多いなど、とても健康的です。₃高血圧や₄糖尿病、₅肥満にもなりにくいベジタリアンになることを、あなたも真剣に考えてみませんか。

Some people say that it is natural to eat meat, but eating meat is linked to various cancers, heart disease and so on. On the other hand, the benefits of a vegetarian diet are well established. A vegetarian diet is low in fat and cholesterol, and high in fiber. Vegetarians have good health with low rates of high blood pressure, diabetes, and obesity (or overweight).

1. 心臓病（　　　　　）（　　　　　）　　4. 糖尿病（　　　　　　　）

2. ベジタリアンの日常の食事（　　　）（　　　）　5. 肥満（　　　　　　　）

3. 高血圧（　　　）（　　　）（　　　）

Listening 🎧16

CD を聴いて、イラストの説明として適切なものを a ～ d から選びましょう。

a.　b.　c.　d.

(KINKO TAMAMAKI)

======= Who needs meat? =======

　Isn't it natural to eat meat? Isn't meat an essential part of a healthy diet? Tim Key and colleagues at the Imperial Cancer Research Fund's Cancer Epidemiology Unit in Oxford, U.K. answered "no" to these questions. They analyzed an enormous amount of research on vegetarian diets — and found great evidence of their beneficial health effects.

5　They compared the mortality rates over 10 years of 76,000 men and women, of whom 28,000 were vegetarians. Meat-eaters, they found, were 24 percent more likely than vegetarians to have died from heart disease, including heart attacks, during that time. Other research has confirmed that vegetarians have unusually good health, with a 40 percent lower risk of colon and certain other cancers than meat-eaters, and low rates of
10　heart disease, high blood pressure, diabetes, obesity and kidney stones.

　So what's harmful about meat? N-nitroso compounds in meat are linked to various cancers. For heart disease, fat is the most harmful component of meat, and heme iron (iron derived from blood) is strongly associated with heart disease in middle-aged adults. The health effects of antibiotics, hormones and other chemicals introduced to animals during
15　the farming process are largely unknown.

　On the other hand, the benefits of a vegetarian diet are well established. More than 900 non-nutritive compounds have been identified from plants. These so-called phytochemicals, present in foods from cauliflower to garlic and tomatoes, are thought to prevent and fight various diseases. A vegetarian diet is low in fat and cholesterol. It is also
20　high in fiber, which protects against (and treats) certain cancers and diabetes.

　Many people reading this will recognize the problems with eating meat and the benefits of a vegetarian diet, but will still not stop eating meat. Custom is a second nature. But if you care about your own health, custom had better change soon. One day, instead of vegetarians being asked, "Why don't you eat meat?" meat-eaters will be asked, "Why do
25　you eat meat?"

(By Rowan Hooper, *The Japan Times*, September 2, 2001)

1 Tim Keyらの研究について、ここで述べられている内容と合わないないものを選びましょう。

a. 肉を食べることは健康的ではないと主張した。
b. 彼らの研究機関はイギリスにある。
c. ベジタリアンの日常の食事に関する莫大な量の研究を分析した。
d. 肉を食べることが健康に役立つという証拠を見つけた。

2 ここで述べられている内容と合うものを選びましょう。

a. Tim Keyらは過去10年以上にわたり、総計76,000人、うち男性28,000人の死亡率を比較した。
b. 肉を食べている人が心臓病で死亡する確率は、24%である。
c. ベジタリアンは、肉を食べている人よりも大腸がんなどの病気になる危険性が40%低い。
d. 腎臓結石になる確率だけは、ベジタリアンも肉を食べる人とほとんど変わらない。

3 ここで述べられている内容と合わないものを選びましょう。

a. 肉の中に、癌の原因になっているN-ニトロソ化合物がある。
b. 肉の成分中で心臓病に最も有害なのは、脂肪である。
c. 血液から出されるヘム鉄が、癌の大きな原因である。
d. 家畜を育てる時に与えられている抗生物質やホルモン・化学物質の人体への影響は、あまり分かっていない。

4 ベジタリアンの食事について、ここで述べられている内容と合わないものを選びましょう。

a. 栄養価の高い化合物が900以上も含まれる。
b. 植物化学物質（phytochemicals）はニンニクからも摂取される。
c. 脂肪やコレステロールが少ない。
d. 糖尿病の予防や治療にも役立つ。

5 肉を好む人が肉食をやめない理由として、ここで指摘されているものを選びましょう。

a. 肉が美味しいこと
b. 肉を食べることが習慣になっていること
c. 肉を食べることが健康に悪いと思っていないこと
d. 「どうして肉を食べるの？」と尋ねられた経験がないこと

Grammar

下線部a〜cの中で語法が誤っているものを選び、訂正しましょう。

1. Currently one _aon three people in the U.K. will develop cancer _bat some time _cin their lives.

    [　] → _____

2. One of the most convincing demonstrations of the _apower of a diet free _bof animal products _ccome from the Coronary Health Improvement Program in the U. S.

    [　] → _____

Vocabulary

A. 下線部に入る適切な語をa〜cから選びましょう。

1. A paper in *The Journal of Clinical Pathology* suggests why vegetables might provide such good health _____.
    a. demerits   b. faults   c. benefits

2. Five hundred people in the program _____ from heart disease or other health problems were cured with a vegetarian diet.
    a. reaching   b. suffering   c. accomplishing

3. The older generations in Japan are in better health with less _____ than the younger, westernized generations raised on burgers.
    a. cholesterol   b. fiber   c. fruits

B. この Unit のトピックに関わる 1〜7 の基本語句について、対応する英語を枠内から選んで記入しましょう。

1. 日常の食事　　（　　　　　　）
2. 死亡率　　　　（　　　　　　）
3. 心臓発作　　　（　　　　　　）
4. 腎臓結石　　　（　　　　　　）
5. 繊維　　　　　（　　　　　　）
6. 抗生物質　　　（　　　　　　）
7. 脂肪　　　　　（　　　　　　）

```
antibiotic
mortality rate
diet
fat
kidney stone
heart attack
fiber
```

Unit 9 さぁ、笑って笑って！

Orientation

枠内の下線部 1 ～ 5 は英語で何というでしょうか。下記の英文を参考にして、対応する語句を書き出しましょう。

> 笑うことで幸せな気持ちになれますが、「1笑い」の効果はそれだけではないようです。例えば、がん細胞を破壊する力のあるリンパ球である2ナチュラルキラー（NK）細胞の活動にも関わりがあると考えられています。この点に注目し、がん3患者のNK細胞を4強化したり、5自然治癒力を高める目的で、楽しいスピーチを聞く月例会を運営している医師もいます。

A physician organizes a monthly session at which patients deliver short, humorous speeches to make other cancer patients and their relatives laugh. He says a good laugh strengthens natural killer cells and natural healing power.

1. 笑い（　　　　　　　　）
2. ナチュラルキラー細胞（　　　）（　　　）（　　　）
3. 患者（　　　　　　　　）
4. 強化する（　　　　　　　　）
5. 自然治癒力（　　　）（　　　）（　　　）

Listening 🎧 18

CDを聴いて、写真の説明として適切なものをa～dから選びましょう。

(AFP－Jiji)

a.　　b.　　c.　　d.

Laughter prescription for good health

Had a good laugh lately? Researchers agree that laughter is not only a lubricant in human relations but, more importantly, can fight disease. As Yoshiko Yanagawa opened her speech with the following lines, her audience roared with laughter: "The only kind of *gan* I knew was the bird. I never dreamed that it would build a nest in the drooping breast of a 60-year-old woman such as myself."

Yanagawa played with the Japanese word "*gan*," which can mean either cancer or wild goose. She had surgery for breast cancer a year ago. She was speaking to 50 cancer patients and their relatives in late March at a monthly "meaning-of-life therapy" session. At each session, patients deliver short, humorous speeches.

The program is organized by Jiro Itami, a physician at Shibata Hospital in Kurashiki, Okayama Prefecture. "When patients dwell on their illness, their anxieties grow," he said. "But by trying to find something funny for their speeches, they look outside themselves in a positive way. A good laugh strengthens natural killer (NK) cells and enhances natural healing power."

NK cells are a kind of lymphocyte that controls the immune system. They can destroy cancer cells and viruses that trigger diseases. To see how laughter affects the activity of NK cells, Itami took 19 cancer patients to the Namba Grand Kagetsu Theater in Osaka. They watched *manzai* (standup comedy) for three hours. He then took blood samples and compared them with samples taken before the show. The level of NK activity showed an increase in 14 patients.

Studies here and overseas show mental stress negatively affects the activity of NK cells. Cancer patients tend to show a lower NK activity than healthy people. One study shows that among cancer patients, the lower the activity of NK cells, the lower the survival rate. Why laughing boosts the activity of NK cells remains a mystery.

(*The Asahi Shimbun*, July 14, 2001)

1 ここで述べられてる内容と合わないものを選びましょう。
a. 笑うことは人間関係の潤滑油となる。
b. 笑うことで病気と闘える。
c. 研究者は、病気との闘いに「笑い」が役に立つと考えている。
d. ヤナガワさんは60歳になるまで、雁（ガン）が巣を作る様子を見たことがなかった。

2 この女性について、ここで述べられている内容と合うものを選びましょう。
a. 彼女は「ガン」という言葉を「銃」の意味で使い、シャレを言った。
b. 彼女はスピーチをした1年前に、肺がんの手術を受けた。
c. 彼女はスピーチをした年の3月にがんの手術を受けた。
d. 彼女は多くのがん患者の前で、自分の体験をユーモラスに語った。

3 伊丹医師が話した内容として、ここで述べられていないものを選びましょう。
a. 患者が自分の病気についてよく考えることによって、不安は克服されていく。
b. 患者は他の患者のスピーチを楽しもうとすることで、前向きに物事を考える。
c. 笑うことでNK細胞の活動が活発になる。
d. 笑うことで自然治癒力が高まる。

4 ここで述べられている内容と合わないものを選びましょう。
a. NK細胞は免疫システムに関係のあるリンパ球である。
b. 笑いがNK細胞に与える効果を調べるため、医者は19人の患者に漫才を見せた。
c. 医師は、漫才を見た患者と見なかった患者の血液中のNK細胞を比べた。
d. 漫才を見た3分の2以上の患者のNK細胞の働きが活発になった。

5 ここで述べられている内容と合わないものを選びましょう。
a. 精神的なストレスがあると、NK細胞の働きが悪くなる。
b. がん患者の方が健康な人よりNK細胞の働きが悪い。
c. がん患者はNK細胞の働きが悪いほど生存率も低くなる。
d. 笑うことによってNK細胞の働きが活発になる仕組みは、すでに解明されている。

Grammar

下線部a～cの中で語法が誤っているものを選び、訂正しましょう。

1. There could be a considerable difference _abetween people who _blaugh a lot and _cone who don't.

    [　] → _____

2. Laughter strongly stimulates the sympathetic nerves, which _aboosts the blood _bflow to the muscles. As a result, the level of brain activity is _cincreased.

    [　] → _____

Vocabulary

A. 下線部に入る適切な語をa～cから選びましょう。

1. In the United States, some hospitals require nurses to make their _____ laugh once a day.
    a. pace makers   b. patients   c. psychiatry

2. Doctors are still studying how NK cells _____ to stimulation.
    a. collect   b. select   c. react

3. Amusing, pleasant laughter _____ heartbeat and breathing and relaxes people.
    a. stabilizes   b. makes   c. stops

B. この Unit のトピックに関わる1～7の基本語句について、対応する英語を枠内から選んで記入しましょう。

1. 生存率　　　　　(　　　　　　　)
2. 乳がん　　　　　(　　　　　　　)
3. 免疫システム　　(　　　　　　　)
4. 精神的ストレス　(　　　　　　　)
5. ウイルス　　　　(　　　　　　　)
6. 外科手術　　　　(　　　　　　　)
7. 高める　　　　　(　　　　　　　)

> immune system
> enhance
> survival rate
> breast cancer
> surgery
> virus
> mental stress

Unit 10 長寿の秘密を教えましょう

Orientation

枠内の下線部 1 ～ 5 は英語で何というでしょうか。下記の英文を参考にして、対応する語句を書き出しましょう。

> 日本人は、今や世界で最も平均寿命が長いといわれています。寿命をさらに延ばすことは可能なのでしょうか。最近、テロメアと呼ばれる1染色体の末端部分が2老化のカギを握っているようだということが分かってきました。3細胞が4分裂するたびにテロメアは短くなり、ある5長さになると細胞は分裂をやめます。それが細胞の死です。

　　The human body is made up of cells, and those cells go on dividing themselves to form new cells. If there were no end to this process, our body could stay young forever. But there is a limit to the number of times a cell can divide itself. Recent research has found that aging results from the shortening of telomeres, which are found at the end of chromosomes. After the telomeres become a certain length, the cells stop dividing.

1. 染色体（　　　　　　　　　）　　4. 分裂する（　　　　　　　　　）
2. 老化（　　　　　　　　　）　　　5. 長さ（　　　　　　　　　）
3. 細胞（　　　　　　　　　）

Listening 🎧 20

CD を聴いて、グラフの説明として適切なものを a ～ d から選びましょう。

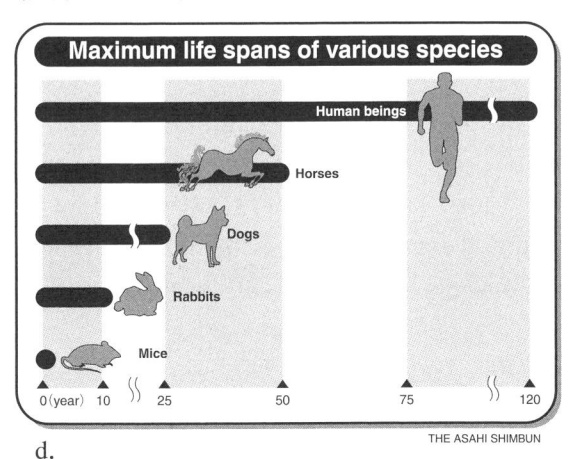

Maximum life spans of various species

- Human beings
- Horses
- Dogs
- Rabbits
- Mice

0 (year)　10　25　50　75　120

THE ASAHI SHIMBUN

a.　　b.　　c.　　d.

Ever-growing life span

Eva Morris, a British woman listed in the Guinness book of records as the longest living woman, died at the age of 114 in November 1999. She apparently died of natural causes. Scientifically speaking, humans can live for up to 120 years. Species have extended their life spans in the process of evolution. But many die from a lack of food or are killed by predators. It is still rare for humans to reach the age of 100.

Even if mankind overcomes the three most common causes of death — cancer, heart disease and stroke — humans will only be able to live 15 years longer, according to a U.S. research team. Why do species age? The answer to that question may lie in what are called telomeres, found at the ends of chromosomes. Telomeres become shorter and shorter after each cell division. After they become a certain length, the cell stops dividing. They die.

But scientists have discovered an enzyme, called telomerase, that lengthens telomeres. Using this enzyme, a group of scientists at the University of Texas announced in 1998 that they have succeeded in making human cells live longer. Some immortal cells, however, do not have telomerase, and some mortal cells have been found to have the enzyme, according to Yoji Mitsui, senior researcher of the National Institute of Bioscience Human-Technology.

Mitsui and his colleagues compared mortal and immortal cells and found a gene that may be related to a cell's life span. "We found that, be it telomeres or the genes we found, neither can explain the principles of longevity alone. We assume the telomeres and genes work together." As society begins to age, research on life spans, aging and medicine for the elderly will advance.

Dr. Leonard Heyflick of the University of California in San Francisco claimed in the 1960s that there is a limit to cell division. Thus, he established the fundamentals of aging research. Now, Heyflick warns that anti-aging treatments trigger many social problems, and that researchers should not aim to achieve such goals. "The most ideal study is for researchers to enable people to live 95 or 100 years using their physical and mental capacity to their utmost."

(*Asahi Evening News*, January 1-2, 2001)

1 ギネスブックに載った長寿世界一の女性の死亡原因を選びましょう。
a. 肉食獣に襲われたこと
b. 餓死
c. 自然死
d. 医療ミス

2 人間の寿命を延ばすために、がん・心臓病・卒中を克服すること以上に効果があると考えられることを選びましょう。
a. 染色体の端にあるテロメアの長さをできるだけ短くする。
b. 細胞分裂を加速する。
c. 細胞分裂を止める。
d. ある基準よりもテロメアが短くなりすぎないように保つ。

3 ここで述べられている内容と合わないものを選びましょう。
a. テロメラーゼという酵素はテロメアを長くする。
b. テロメラーゼという酵素を用いて、人間の細胞をより長く生かすことに成功した科学者たちがいる。
c. 三井研究員によると、不死性細胞の中にテロメラーゼを持っていないものがある一方で、死ぬ細胞でもテロメラーゼを持っているものがある。
d. すべての細胞はテロメラーゼを持っている。

4 ここで述べられている内容と合うものを選びましょう。
a. 三井研究員は、死ぬ細胞の研究だけを行った。
b. 三井研究員は、寿命を延ばすのに関係しているのはテロメアではなく遺伝子だと述べている。
c. 三井研究員は、テロメアと遺伝子の両方が長寿に関連していると考えている。
d. 将来は、特に若者に対する医療が進んでいくだろう。

5 Heyflick博士の研究活動について、ここで述べられている内容と合わないものを選びましょう。
a. 細胞分裂の数には制限があるということを発見した。
b. 老化を防ぐ治療が多くの社会問題の引き金になると警告している。
c. 人々がそれぞれの肉体的・精神的能力を最大限に生かして、1世紀近く生きることを可能にする研究が理想的であると述べた。
d. 研究者は今後、老化を防ぐ治療法開発に最も力を注ぐべきである、と述べている。

Grammar

下線部a~cの中で語法が誤っているものを選び、訂正しましょう。

1. _aBe it his order _bor request, I will accept it _cin pleasure.

    [　] → _____

2. _aThe elderly will comprise an _bestimate 26 percent of the population _cby 2025.

    [　] → _____

Vocabulary

A. 下線部に入る適切な語をa~cから選びましょう。

1. The _____ cell cannot reproduce. It has to die.
    a. mortal   b. physical   c. longer

2. Cells go on _____ themselves to form new cells.
    a. aging   b. living   c. dividing

3. An _____ is a chemical substance that is found in living creatures which produces changes in other substances without being changed itself.
    a. enzyme   b. oxygen   c. element

B. このUnitのトピックに関わる1~7の基本語句について、対応する英語を枠内から選んで記入しましょう。

1. 平均寿命   (   )
2. 肉食獣   (   )
3. 酵素   (   )
4. 社会問題   (   )
5. 不死の   (   )
6. 長寿   (   )
7. 遺伝子   (   )

```
social problem
gene
enzyme
predator
average life span
longevity
immortal
```

Unit 11　"秋バテ"退治法

Orientation

枠内の下線部1〜5は英語で何というでしょうか。下記の英文を参考にして、対応する語句を書き出しましょう。

> 年々、「秋バテ」を訴える若い₁サラリーマンが増えています。東京都渋谷区のある₂神経・精神科医院の医師によると、₃疲労、₄食欲減退、勤労₅意欲の喪失などが主な症状だということです。その原因として、一般的には夏の暑さが考えられていますが、果たしてそれだけでしょうか。

　　Every September, young salaried workers visit a neuropsychiatric clinic in Shibuya Ward, Tokyo, complaining of exhaustion, loss of appetite and a lack of motivation to work. The clinic director says the symptoms are typical of "akibate."

1. サラリーマン（　　　　）（　　　　）
2. 神経・精神科医院（　　　　）（　　　　）
3. 疲労（　　　　　　　　）
4. 食欲減退（　　　）（　　　）（　　　）
5. 意欲（　　　　　　　）

Listening 🎧 22

CDを聴いて、写真の説明として適切なものをa〜dから選びましょう。

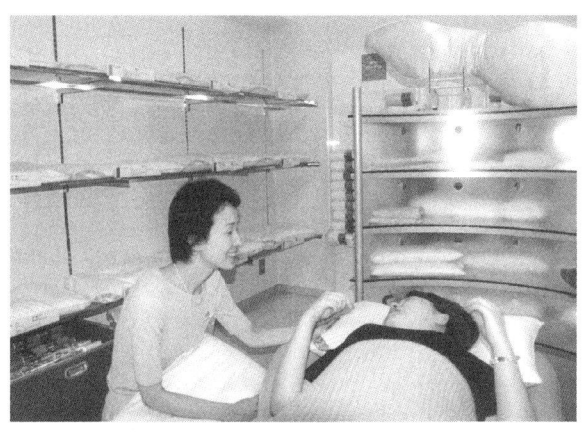

（読売新聞社）

a.　　b.　　c.　　d.

Keeping regular hours can prevent "akibate"

"*Akibate*," often brought on by the lingering heat of summer, leaves people feeling run-down. But heat exhaustion isn't the only cause. People who are confined to overly air-conditioned rooms, take cold drinks but skip meals, oversleep or stay up all night during the summer are also prone to the condition.

Sekiya, a director of Hatsudai Clinic, proposes the following ways to overcome *akibate*. Eat meals rich in vitamins and proteins instead of relying on cold drinks and food. Exercise during the day and take warm baths in the evening. Get a good night's sleep. Although proper sleep is one of the best ways to overcome *akibate*, it can be difficult for busy people to maintain regular sleep patterns.

One of the keys to understanding the mechanism of sleep patterns is to learn how body temperature affects the rhythm of daily life. People feel lethargic in the mornings when body temperatures are at their lowest, and become most active in the evenings when body temperatures peak.

It takes 25 hours for body temperatures to complete their cycle, so one hour is carried over into the next day. These "leftover" hours accumulate and people who keep late hours during the summer may find it difficult to wake up in the mornings. However, exposure to sunlight in the mornings can help shorten the cycle to fit into the 24-hour day.

A scientist notes that it takes at least one week for late risers to get into this 24-hour pattern. A neat bedroom and clean bedding, in addition to stretching and listening to music before going to bed, can help people achieve a good night's sleep. Scented bed sprays can also be calming.

(*The Daily Yomiuri*, September 8, 2001)

1 秋バテの原因として、ここで指摘されていないものを選びましょう。

a. 冷房の効きすぎた部屋にいること
b. きちんと食事をせず、冷たい飲み物ばかりを飲むこと
c. 夏の間中、運動をしすぎること
d. 夏の間中、夜更かしをすること

2 秋バテを克服する方法として、ここで述べられていないものを選びましょう。

a. 暑い日中に昼寝をすること
b. ビタミンやタンパク質を豊富に含んだ食物を摂取すること
c. 日中に運動をしたあと、夕方に温かい風呂に入ること
d. 夜、睡眠を十分とること

3 体温と体調の関係について、ここで述べられている内容と合うものを選びましょう。

a. 体調と体温の上昇・低下は関係がない。
b. 朝に体温が頂点に達するので、人は最も倦怠感を感じる。
c. 朝に体温が最も下がるので、人は最も元気になる。
d. 夕方に体温が頂点に達するので、人は最も元気になる。

4 体温の周期について、ここで述べられている内容と合うものを選びましょう。

a. １周期が25時間なので、翌日の周期は１時間短くなる。
b. 朝、日光を浴びないと、周期はどんどん翌日へずれ込んでいく。
c. 周期は、生活パターンにかかわらず常に一定である。
d. 朝のうちに日光を浴びると、周期が短くなりすぎて不安定になる。

5 安眠するための方法として、ここで述べられていないものを選びましょう。

a. 気持ちのよい寝具をととのえること
b. 寝る前に手足を伸ばしたり、音楽を聴くこと
c. ベッドをよい香りで包むこと
d. 温かい飲み物を飲むこと

Grammar

下線部a～cの中で語法が誤っているものを選び、訂正しましょう。

1. The doctor _aadvises his patients _bto keep regular _chour.

    [ ] → _____

2. It is better to get up _aat about the same time on holidays as on weekdays, catch some _bsunlights and _chave breakfast.

    [ ] → _____

Vocabulary

A. 下線部に入る適切な語をa～cから選びましょう。

1. In order to keep regular hours, some salaried workers choose to live at company _____.
    a. warehouses   b. dormitories   c. factories

2. People should eat breakfast to _____ their bodies.
    a. energy   b. energetic   c. energize

3. People who wake up late in the morning on weekends often feel _____ the following Monday.
    a. run-down   b. run-off   c. run-out

B. この Unit のトピックに関わる１～７の基本語句について、対応する英語を枠内から選んで記入しましょう。

1. 夜更かしする　　（　　　　　　）
2. 元気にする　　　（　　　　　　）
3. 体調が悪い　　　（　　　　　　）
4. （心身を）静める（　　　　　　）
5. タンパク質　　　（　　　　　　）
6. ～に依存する　　（　　　　　　）
7. たまる　　　　　（　　　　　　）

rely on
accumulate
keep late hours
calming
energize
feel run-down
protein

Unit 12 若い者には負けません

Orientation

枠内の下線部 1 ～ 5 は英語で何というでしょうか。下記の英文を参考にして、対応する語句を書き出しましょう。

> かつて₁高齢者は「病気がちである」とか「非生産的である」と考えられがちでした。しかし寿命が延びた今、このような決まりきった見方をせず、高齢者の₂潜在能力を高め、社会に貢献してもらうことが大変重要になってきています。そのため昨今、「₃老化防止医学」が推奨されています。これは、あらゆる医学の₄専門分野を統合し、遺伝子治療のような₅先端技術を駆使するものです。一方、医師は単に医療を行うだけでなく、健康面での患者のパートナーになることが必要となっています。

The new field of antiaging medicine, which integrates the "best" of every medical specialty and essentially employs advanced technology, is now being promoted. With longer life spans, it is now very important to enhance the potential of the elderly, who are often dismissed as sickly and unproductive, and to enable them to make more meaningful contributions to society.

1. 高齢者（   ）（   ）
2. 潜在能力（   ）
3. 老化防止医学（   ）（   ）
4. 専門分野（   ）
5. 先端技術（   ）（   ）

Listening 〔CD 24〕

CD を聴いて、写真の説明として適切なものを a ～ d から選びましょう。

a.　　b.　　c.　　d.

（毎日新聞社）

Doctors prescribe antiaging therapy

A U.S. doctor promoting the new field of antiaging medicine said that the public should do away with stereotypes of the elderly as sickly and unproductive and think instead of extending life's "usable years." "Today's 60-year-old is like yesterday's 40-year-old," Robert Goldman, chairman of the American Academy of Anti-Aging Medicine, said. "We have to change our perception of what is old."

According to the doctor, antiaging medicine refers to the concept of optimizing and integrating the "best" of every medical specialty, and making patients and doctors interact in a more proactive way by enabling doctors to make a difference in their patients' lives. A doctor goes beyond being a mere "health-care provider" by acting as a "facilitator and partner in health with their patients."

The doctor said antiaging medicine, which takes after sports medicine, essentially employs advanced technology — including hormone replacement therapy, nutritional intervention and gene therapy — to detect, prevent, and intervene in age-related diseases.

Citing the case of seniors in the United States who are involved in voluntary work or teaching at universities, Goldman lauded their efforts by saying, "The wisdom and input and the guidance that these people can give is enormous."

With longer life spans, it is now imperative to enhance and maximize the potential of the elderly, who are often dismissed as having no purpose, and enable them to make more meaningful contributions to society, Goldman said. "The world cannot afford not to make antiaging medicine one of the mainstream areas in the field of medicine," he said.

('*Kyodo News,*' *The Japan Times*, November 10, 2001)

1 ここで述べられている内容と合わないものを選びましょう。
a. 「高齢者というのは病気がちである」という型にはまった認識を捨てるべきである。
b. 高齢者が非生産的であるという事実は認識しておかなければならない。
c. 今の60歳は一昔前の40歳といえる。
d. 「高齢である」ということの認識を改めなければならない。

2 「老化防止医学」について、ここで述べられている内容と合わないものを選びましょう。
a. あらゆる医学専門分野の最高の部分を統合するものである。
b. 医師と患者がより前向きな関係を築いていくものである。
c. 医師は従来の医療行為をまったく行わない。
d. 医師は患者の健康を促進するよきパートナーとしての役割を担っている。

3 「老化防止医学」について、ここで述べられている内容と合わないものを選びましょう。
a. スポーツ医学に似ている。
b. 先端技術は使わず、自然療法を用いる。
c. ホルモン置換治療や栄養面での介入・遺伝子治療を行う。
d. 加齢に関係した病気を発見したり、その予防や介入を行う。

4 アメリカの高齢者の活動として、ここで述べられている内容と合わないものを選びましょう。
a. ボランテイア活動をする。
b. 大学で教鞭をとる。
c. 自分の知恵や指導力を使って努力する。
d. ベンチャービジネスを始める。

5 ここで述べられている内容と合うものを選びましょう。
a. 高齢者の潜在力を高めることが非常に重要である。
b. 社会に貢献できる高齢者はほとんどいない。
c. 世界が足並みをそろえて老化防止医学を研究することはできない。
d. 老化防止医学を医学の主流にすることはできない。

Grammar

下線部a～cの中で語法が誤っているものを選び、訂正しましょう。

1. Years _atill now, Europe and the world _bwill move _con to the preventive model of medicine in the future.

    [　] → _____

2. _aClaiming that medical knowledge doubles _beach 3 $1/2$ years, Goldman said, "You don't know what _cwill happen next, but one thing you can count on is change."

    [　] → _____

Vocabulary

A. 下線部に入る適切な語をa～cから選びましょう。

1. Japan cannot afford to have millions of people that are sick and incapable of _____ for themselves.
    a. waking   b. caring   c. educating

2. Look at the _____ and genius we lose when someone dies.
    a. wisdom   b. poverty   c. age

3. Antiaging medicine can slow down the aging process to _____ healthier lives for the elderly.
    a. stop   b. decrease   c. enable

B. このUnitのトピックに関わる1～7の基本語句について、対応する英語を枠内から選んで記入しましょう。

1. 高齢者　　　　　(　　　　　　)
2. 老化防止の　　　(　　　　　　)
3. 加齢に伴う　　　(　　　　　　)
4. 介入　　　　　　(　　　　　　)
5. 予防する　　　　(　　　　　　)
6. スポーツ医学　　(　　　　　　)
7. 貢献　　　　　　(　　　　　　)

> sports medicine
> prevent
> contribution
> intervention
> senior
> age-related
> antiaging

Unit 13 はた迷惑な客──電磁波

Orientation

枠内の下線部 1 ～ 5 は英語で何というでしょうか。下記の英文を参考にして、対応する語句を書き出しましょう。

> 電磁₁放射物が人間に対して悪影響を与えるということは、以前から専門家によって指摘されています。それにもかかわらず、東京の下町のど真ん中に₂携帯電話の₃通信塔を建てる計画が持ち上がりました。住民たちは、₄電磁波が引き起こすかもしれない₅健康障害を心配し、計画に対して憤激しています。

Plans for a cell phone communications tower in an older area of Tokyo have driven locals into a fury over the health hazards posed by the electromagnetic waves. Experts say that electromagnetic emissions have an adverse effect on humans.

1. 放射物（　　　　　　　　　）　　4. 電磁波（　　　　　）（　　　　　）

2. 携帯電話（　　　　）（　　　　）　5. 健康障害（　　　　）（　　　　）

3. 通信塔（　　　　　）（　　　　）

Listening 26

CD を聴いて、写真の説明として適切なものを a ～ d から選びましょう。

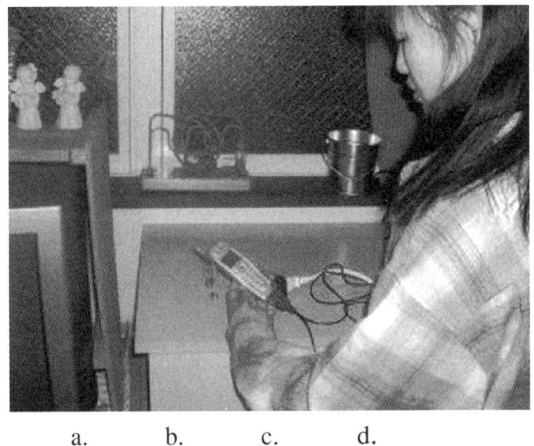

a.　　b.　　c.　　d.

Towers suffer wave of protest over health risks

NTT DoCoMo wants to build a communications tower atop a 27 story-high skyscraper on a plot of land in Tokyo's Sumida Ward. Officials from NTT DoCoMo say the tower is necessary to cope with the flood of signals stemming from the growing popularity of mobile phones. They also say the tower will improve the sound quality of mobile phones and will help the company prepare for the introduction of next-generation mobile phones.

NTT DoCoMo initially planned to construct only a high-rise office building. Residents learned of the company's plan to erect a communications tower atop the facility at a meeting in September last year. Prompted by anger at the company's unexpected change of plan, residents formed a group to demand the company to review the tower's construction.

But NTT DoCoMo officials reject residents' claims that they will be bombarded by potentially dangerous electromagnetic emissions. They argue few waves will reach the bottom of the building since the antenna is located on top of the tower and electromagnetic signals travel horizontally.

The building near the north exit of JR Ryogoku Station is scheduled for completion by the end of fiscal 2003. Residents have collected the signatures of 9,000 people opposed to the tower's construction and are considering making a complaint with the Tokyo metropolitan government's mediation committee.

The old Posts and Telecommunications Ministry in October, 1999, established the maximum safe human exposure level to electromagnetic waves, which officials say is equal to the level set by the World Health Organization. The ministry does not oppose construction of communications towers so long as the level of electromagnetic emissions is below the WHO standard.

(*The International Herald Tribune Asahi*, September 1-2, 2001)

1 通信塔について、NTT DoCoMoの幹部がここで述べている内容と合わないものを選びましょう。
  a. 通信塔は、携帯電話から発信される電磁信号の「洪水」に対処するために必要である。
  b. 通信塔は、携帯電話の音質を改善する。
  c. 通信塔が建てば、次世代携帯電話を導入する準備が可能になる。
  d. 通信塔と住民の健康はまったく関係がない。

2 住民がNTT DoCoMoに対して最も怒っている理由を選びましょう。
  a. 高層のビルを建てようとしているから。
  b. 通信塔の建設計画を途中でつけ加えたから。
  c. 住民に対する事前説明会を開かなかったから。
  d. 会社の計画に反対する住民グループの結成を妨害するから。

3 NTT DoCoMoが「通信塔には危険がない」とする理由を選びましょう。
  a. 電磁放射物は潜在的には危険がないから。
  b. 電磁信号の大部分はビルの下部に到達するから。
  c. 電磁信号のほとんどはアンテナと同じ高さを伝わり、地上には影響がないから。
  d. 電磁信号は地上波であるから。

4 この建設計画に反対して住民が起こした行動を選びましょう。
  a. 別の通信塔を建てた。
  b. 通信塔の建設に反対する住民の署名を集めた。
  c. デモ行進をした。
  d. 調停委員会に苦情を申し出た。

5 1999年10月より前に最大安全被ばく値を定めた機関・団体を選びましょう。
  a. 旧郵政省
  b. 世界保健機関
  c. NTT DoCoMo
  d. 住民団体

Grammar

下線部a～cの中で語法が誤っているものを選び、訂正しましょう。

1. Company officials say that designs _afor the tower _bmeets central _cgovernment-designated criteria.

    [ ] → _____

2. Those _aopposing the tower construction cite the fact _bwhich the area is home to numerous public facilities, _cincluding several schools and a hospital.

    [ ] → _____

Vocabulary

A. 下線部に入る適切な語をa～cから選びましょう。

1. There is no denying that electromagnetic waves have an _____ effect on humans.
    a. energetic   b. adverse   c. informal

2. A mother of a student at a school _____ to the site explained the situation.
    a. adjacent   b. address   c. additional

3. Strong local opposition forced Tu-ka Cellular Tokyo to _____ plans to construct a communications tower in Saitama Prefecture.
    a. happen   b. hurry   c. halt

B. このUnitのトピックに関わる1～7の基本語句について、対応する英語を枠内から選んで記入しましょう。

1. 携帯電話   (   )
2. 基準   (   )
3. 水平に   (   )
4. 完成   (   )
5. 調停委員会   (   )
6. 被ばく   (   )
7. 住民   (   )

> exposure
> horizontally
> mobile phone
> completion
> mediation committee
> resident
> criteria

Unit 14 副作用が知りたい！

Orientation

枠内の下線部1〜5は英語で何というでしょうか。下記の英文を参考にして、対応する語句を書き出しましょう。

> 心臓病や脳卒中の原因になるコレステロール値を下げる₁薬バイコールは、₂認可されたとき、₃副作用がほとんど無いと考えられていました。しかし、患者の筋肉が破壊され、死に至ることもあるという重大な副作用が発見されたため、₄処方する際に₅予防措置を講じるよう、医師に対して警告がなされました。しかし、医師はこの警告に留意しなかったため、バイコールは市場から消えることになりました。それ以降、医師への警告体制強化が大いに求められています。

When a drug called Baycol was approved, it appeared to have few side effects. Later, doctors were warned to take precautions when prescribing it because serious side effects had been seen. The warnings, however, failed to settle the problem.

1. 薬（　　　　　　　　　）　　4. 処方する（　　　　　　　　　）

2. 認可する（　　　　　　　　）　5. 予防措置（　　　　　　　　　）

3. 副作用（　　　　）（　　　　）

Listening 28

CDを聴いて、写真の説明として適切なものをa〜dから選びましょう。

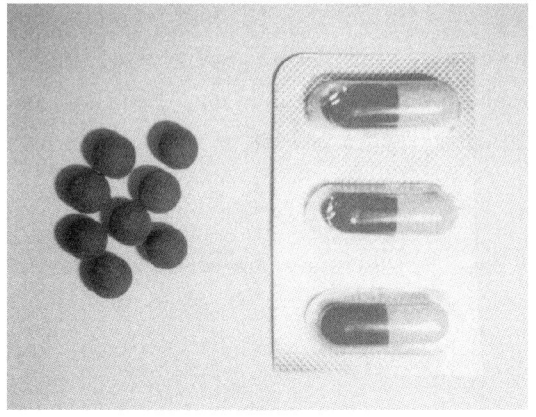

a.　　b.　　c.　　d.

Warnings about drugs go unheeded

When Baycol, a cholesterol-lowering drug, was approved in 1997, it appeared to be a potentially lifesaving drug with few side effects. It had been tested on more than 3,000 patients, and no serious problems had turned up. Baycol was one of a class of powerful anti-cholesterol drugs that save thousands of lives by preventing heart attacks and strokes.

But on Aug. 8, Baycol was taken off the market. Its manufacturer, Bayer AG of Germany, took that step after 31 patients on the drug had died and the cases cast suspicion on Baycol. The deaths were caused by a disorder in which muscle cells break down, flooding the kidneys with masses of cellular waste. Death occurs if the kidneys are overwhelmed and shut down.

Experts say the story of Baycol shows the kind of communication failure that has occurred before and may well occur again with other drugs. When muscle problems and deaths linked to Baycol were reported, Bayer and the U.S. Food and Drug Administration warned doctors to take precautions in prescribing the drug, but the warnings failed to settle the problem, and Baycol finally had to be taken off the market.

Last week in *The Journal of the American Medical Association*, FDA doctors published a study based on the case of a diabetes drug called Rezulin. As a few reports associating Rezulin with liver failure came in, the federal drug agency and the drug's maker sent four separate warning letters to doctors. The FDA study showed that most doctors did not heed the message.

Problems with warnings that go unheeded would continue and might multiply in the future. "This will keep happening as medicine gets more advanced and drugs that are very helpful, but have unexpected problems, come along," Dr. Thorn of Brigham and Women's Hospital said. A more effective warning system is needed to alert doctors to drug side effects and problems.

(*The International Herald Tribune Asahi*, August 23, 2001)

1 バイコールについて、ここで述べられている内容と合うものを選びましょう。
a. 認可された時、数種の副作用があることはすでに判明していた。
b. 臨床試験は、認可前にはまったく行われていなかった。
c. 臨床試験では、深刻な問題は何も見つからなかった。
d. 認可されたのは、頭痛にも大変効果があったからである。

2 ここで述べられていないものを選びましょう。
a. バイコールは8月8日に市場から回収された。
b. バイコールを製造元のバイエル社が回収したのは、服用していた患者が31人亡くなった後だった。
c. 服用患者の死因は、筋肉細胞が壊れ、破壊された細胞で腎臓が満たされたことだった。
d. 服用患者の死因は、肝不全であった。

3 ここで述べられていないものを選びましょう。
a. バイコールが市場回収されるに至った原因は、コミュニケーションの不備である。
b. 他の薬剤についてもコミュニケーションの不備は起こる可能性がある。
c. バイコールによる死亡のケースが報告されたとき、米国食品医薬品局などが、医師に対して予防策をとるように警告した。
d. 警告を受けた後、医師はようやくバイコールを処方する際の予防策をとるようになった。

4 薬剤レズリンについて、ここで述べられていないものを選びましょう。
a. 糖尿病の薬である。
b. 副作用として、肝障害を引き起こす疑いがある。
c. 副作用が判明したとき、医師に警告書が送られた。
d. ほとんどの医師は、この薬の副作用について熟知していた。

5 ここで述べられている内容と合うものを選びましょう。
a. 副作用について警告されても医師が注意を払わない状態は、今後も続くであろう。
b. 医学が進歩するにつれて、医師は副作用の警告にますます注意を払うようになるだろう。
c. 医薬開発が進歩するにつれて、予期しない副作用の問題はなくなるであろう。
d. 薬品の副作用について医師に警告する体制は万全である。

Grammar

下線部a～cの中で語法が誤っているものを選び、訂正しましょう。

1. The European Medicine Evaluation Agency a have said that it b would review its warnings c for the drugs.

    [　] → _____

2. Problems a with Baycol had become apparent b by December 1999, more than two c year after it went on the market.

    [　] → _____

Vocabulary

A. 下線部に入る適切な語をa～cから選びましょう。

1. The FDA asked doctors to order liver tests for _____ taking the drug.
    a. patients   b. nurses   c. surgeons

2. A little more than a year later, the second _____ was sent to doctors.
    a. warning   b. side effect   c. muscle

3. Doctors were _____ not to give patients drug A and drug B at the same time.
    a. prevented   b. promised   c. advised

B. この Unit のトピックに関わる1～7の基本語句について、対応する英語を枠内から選んで記入しましょう。

1. 警告する　　　　(　　　　　　　)
2. 疑惑　　　　　　(　　　　　　　)
3. 気をつける　　　(　　　　　　　)
4. 筋肉　　　　　　(　　　　　　　)
5. 肝不全　　　　　(　　　　　　　)
6. 効果のある　　　(　　　　　　　)
7. 命を救う　　　　(　　　　　　　)

```
suspicion
effective
liver failure
heed
muscle
warn
lifesaving
```

Unit 15 世界初のヒトクローン胚

Orientation

枠内の下線部 1 ～ 5 は英語で何というでしょうか。下記の英文を参考にして、対応する語句を書き出しましょう。

> 1997年、クローン羊ドリーの登場は世界中の人々を驚かせました。また最近、アメリカのある企業が世界で初めてヒトの1クローン2胚作成に成功したことが報じられました。けれども、卵子の3提供者と遺伝子的にまったく同じこの胚について、4医療倫理や法律の観点からさまざまな論議が沸き起こっており、5懐疑的な見方をする科学者も大勢います。

A Massachusetts company, Advanced Cell Technology, declared that it had created the world's first cloned human embryo, an early-stage embryo that genetically was the exact copy of its female donor. The announcement has ignited a storm about medical ethics and research laws. Many scientists are skeptical about the research.

1. クローンの（　　　　　　　）　　4. 医療倫理（　　　　　）（　　　　　）

2. 胚（　　　　　　　）　　5. 懐疑的な（　　　　　　　　）

3. 提供者（　　　　　　　）

Listening 🎧30

CD を聴いて、イラストの説明として適切なものを a ～ d から選びましょう。

a.　b.　c.　d.

(KINKO TAMAMAKI)

Reading 31

First cloned human embryo

Advanced Cell Technology (ACT) told the world to distinguish between reproductive cloning — bringing a clone to term as a baby — and therapeutic cloning, using embryonic master cells to cure diabetes, heart disease, Alzheimer's disease, etc. "Our dream is that someday we could take a patient's skin cell, and give them back anything that they needed to cure disease," said ACT's President Michael West.

Under therapeutic cloning, stem cells which have an ability to grow into any kinds of cells would be taken from an embryo. They would grow into specific cells, such as liver, brain or muscle cells. The specific cells are injected into the patient and grow into fresh and active young tissue. Any transplant that uses donated cells has the risk of tissue rejection. But if a copy of the patient's own cells is used, the risk of rejection should be much smaller.

ACT used two methods to make the clones. One of them is a technique called "nuclear transfer," similar to the method used to create the sheep clone, Dolly. In this method, they take a nucleus of an unfertilized egg and replace it with a nucleus of an adult cell.

The other is the so-called "virgin birth" technique. Under this, the only genetic material used comes from the mother's egg: There is no male sperm. Instead, chemicals are used to stimulate the egg, then the egg starts dividing. ACT's clones are believed to be the first human cells that have been reproduced in this manner.

If the "virgin birth" technique can be made to work, it could help to ease ethical concerns about therapeutic cloning. As no sperm would be used, there would be no fertilization in the traditional sense. And the embryo cannot develop into a baby, because the fetus dies in early development without male genes. Cloning research is a step forward.

('*AFP-Jiji,*' *Japan Times Weekly*, December 8, 2001)

1 ここで述べられている内容と合うものを選びましょう。

a. クローンを妊娠満期（term）まで赤ちゃんとして成長させるものを、治療的クローニングという。
b. 治療的クローニングとは、胚性万能細胞を使って病気の治療を行なうことである。
c. 治療的クローニングでは、心臓病は治せないが、アルツハイマー病は治せる。
d. 患者の皮膚細胞から作り出した細胞を使って病気を治療することは現在でも可能だ。

2 治療的クローニングについて、ここで述べられている内容と合わないものを選びましょう。

a. どのような細胞にも成長できる幹細胞は、胚から取り出される。
b. 取り出された幹細胞を、肝臓や脳などの特定の細胞へと成長させる。
c. 胚から取り出したばかりの幹細胞を患者に注入する。
d. 患者自身の細胞を使ったクローニングなので、拒絶反応の危険性は少ない。

3 「核移植」法について、ここで述べられている内容と合わないものを選びましょう。

a. ACT社が使った2つのクローン技術のうちの1つである。
b. クローン羊ドリーを作った方法と似ている。
c. 未受精卵子から核を抜いて、そこに提供した大人の細胞の核を入れる。
d. 提供した大人の細胞から核を抜いて、そこに未受精卵子の核を入れる。

4 「処女生殖」法について、ここで述べられている内容と合わないものを選びましょう。

a. 使われるのは、母親の卵子の遺伝物質のみである。
b. 男性の精子が使われる。
c. 卵子に分割を始めさせるために、化学物質で卵子を刺激する。
d. ACT社が、世界で初めてヒトの細胞を再生した方法であると考えられる。

5 「処女生殖」法について、ここで述べられている内容と合うものを選びましょう。

a. クローニングに対する倫理的な懸念を大きくする。
b. これまでと同じ意味での受精が起こる。
c. 胚は健康な赤ちゃんへと育つ。
d. 男性の精子が使われず、胎児（胚）は発達の初期段階で死ぬ。

Grammar

下線部a〜cの中で語法が誤っているものを選び、訂正しましょう。

1. ACT published ₐthe research ᵦin an online science journal rather ᴄfor in a prestige publication.

    [　] → _____

2. One of the ₐresearchers said that the ᵦachievements is only a preliminary ᴄobservation.

    [　] → _____

Vocabulary

A. 下線部に入る適切な語をa〜cから選びましょう。

1. The announcement of the world's first cloned human embryo is set to ignite a fresh storm about medical _____ .
    a. colleges   b. ethics   c records

2. The ACT company's _____ have never gone beyond the six-cell stage before dying.
    a. embryos   b. sperms   c. babies

3. Stem _____ are harvested from a clustered ball of more than 100 cells called blastocyte.
    a. eggs   b. embryos   c. cells

B. この Unit のトピックに関わる1〜7の基本語句について、対応する英語を枠内から選んで記入しましょう。

1. 拒絶反応　　　(　　　　　　　)
2. 幹細胞　　　　(　　　　　　　)
3. 核　　　　　　(　　　　　　　)
4. 受精　　　　　(　　　　　　　)
5. 入れ換える　　(　　　　　　　)
6. 胎児　　　　　(　　　　　　　)
7. 治療の　　　　(　　　　　　　)

```
replace
rejection
fertilization
fetus
nucleus
stem cell
therapeutic
```

Unit 16 視力低下にご注意！

Orientation

枠内の下線部 1 〜 5 は英語で何というでしょうか。下記の英文を参考にして、対応する語句を書き出しましょう。

> 年をとると多くの人々が 1 <u>視力</u>の衰えを自覚します。目の奥には 2 <u>網膜</u>という複雑なスクリーンがあり、光を 3 <u>神経インパルス</u>に変換します。そして、脳がこのインパルスを、見たものとして認識するのです。視力の低下は、この網膜の 4 <u>異常</u>と大変関係があります。5 <u>眼科医</u>があなたの目をじっと見つめたからといって、ドキッとする必要はありません。網膜の異常を探しているだけですから。

　　After age 50, eyesight often goes downhill. When the ophthalmologist looks deeply into your eyes, he is not searching for romance but for abnormalities in the retina, the complex "screen" at the back that translates light into nerve impulses, interpreted by our brains as sight.

1. 視力（　　　　　　　　　）　　4. 異常（　　　　　　　　　　　）

2. 網膜（　　　　　　　　　）　　5. 眼科医（　　　　　　　　　　）

3. 神経インパルス（　　　　　）（　　　　　）

Listening 🎧 32

CD を聴いて、写真の説明として適切なものを a 〜 d から選びましょう。

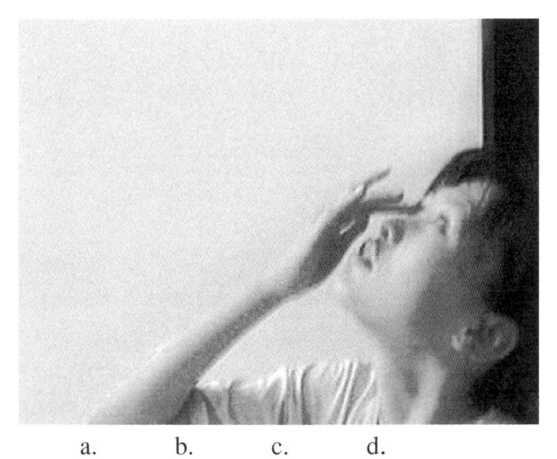

a.　　b.　　c.　　d.

Now you see it, now you don't

The leading cause of permanent loss of sight among the elderly is age-related macular degeneration (AMD). When we look at an object, the image is focused on the macula, a yellowish area around the middle of the retina.

Risk factors for AMD are smoking, advanced age, family history of the disease, history of heart disease, race (predominantly whites), sex (females slightly more often than males), and exposure to ultraviolet light.

We can control some of these. Smokers should quit smoking to encourage healthy circulation throughout the body. If you have high blood pressure or high "bad" cholesterol, follow your doctor's advice about diet and medication. Protect your vision by wearing a hat and eyeglasses or sunglasses with UV-blocking lenses.

Good nutrition seems to help prevent AMD by providing vitamin C and other antioxidants. Strive for a balanced diet. Choose plenty of fruits, green vegetables, whole grains and other unprocessed food. Meat, fish, beans and peas provide zinc, also thought to be beneficial.

Fortunately, there are many aids to help those with low vision. Strong reading glasses, hand magnifiers, magnifiers that fit over reading material, a variety of telescopes, as well as large-print books — all make daily life easier.

(*The Daily Yomiuri*, September 8, 2001)

1 ここで述べられている内容と合わないものを選びましょう。

a. 高齢者が失明する最大の原因は、AMDとよばれる現象である。
b. AMDとは、年齢に比例して黄斑（macula）が退化する現象である。
c. 見られた物の像は、黄斑に焦点が合わされる。
d. 網膜は、黄斑の中央付近にある黄色の部分である。

2 AMDを引き起こしやすい要因として、ここで述べられていないものを選びましょう。

a. 心臓病にかかりやすい家系であること
b. 白色人種であること
c. 女性であること
d. 紫外線に長時間さらされること

3 AMD対策として、ここで述べられていないものを選びましょう。

a. 体内の循環器系を活性化させるために禁煙をする。
b. 血圧や悪玉コレステロールの数値が高いときは、食餌療法や薬物療法について医者に相談する。
c. 常に目が乾かないようにする。
d. 帽子や紫外線カットのサングラスで目を保護する。

4 AMDを防止する栄養物として、ここで述べられていないものを選びましょう。

a. ビタミンCを含んでいる食べ物
b. 酸化を促進する食べ物
c. 加工されていない食べ物
d. 亜鉛を含んでいる食べ物

5 視力の悪い人を助ける製品として、ここで述べられていないものを選びましょう。

a. 度の強い眼鏡
b. 拡大鏡
c. 顕微鏡
d. 活字の大きい本

Grammar

下線部a～cの中で語法が誤っているものを選び、訂正しましょう。

1. _aFocusing on printed _bmaterials is _cincreasing difficult especially in dim light.

   [　] → _____

2. A dark, light or blurred spot _amay appear in the central vision, making _bit difficult _cdrive or even read labels.

   [　] → _____

Vocabulary

A. 下線部に入る適切な語をa～cから選びましょう。

1. _____ of AMD typically develop gradually and in both eyes at once.
   a. Systems　　b. Symptoms　　c. Symbols

2. All treatments for AMD depend on early _____, and none can guarantee complete restoration of sight.
   a. diagnosis　　b. diameter　　c. diagram

3. You should not take this drug if you are _____.
   a. preparatory　　b. permanent　　c. pregnant

B. この Unit のトピックに関わる１～７の基本語句について、対応する英語を枠内から選んで記入しましょう。

1. 紫外線をさえぎる　（　　　　　　）
2. 拡大鏡　　　　　　（　　　　　　）
3. ～の上で焦点が合う（　　　　　　）
4. 亜鉛　　　　　　　（　　　　　　）
5. 薬物療法　　　　　（　　　　　　）
6. 栄養物　　　　　　（　　　　　　）
7. 退化　　　　　　　（　　　　　　）

```
zinc
medication
magnifier
be focused on
degeneration
UV-blocking
nutrition
```

Unit 17 患者を護る——人工心臓移植と代弁人——

Orientation

枠内の下線部 1 ～ 5 は英語で何というでしょうか。下記の英文を参考にして、対応する語句を書き出しましょう。

> 回復の望みが乏しい重症患者の中には、最新の治療法の1医療実験に最後の望みを託して、自らその実験台になる人もいます。しかし、患者は医師に対して2弱い立場にあるため、その実験に伴う危険性について、正確な情報を知らされているとは必ずしも言えません。そこで、世界初の3埋め込み式4人工心臓の移植手術が行われた際、患者の利益を守る「5患者代弁人」の制度が設立されました。

　　Desperate patients sign up for medical experiments, clinging to the thinnest sliver of hope that the latest discovery might save their lives. It is such eagerness that puts vulnerable patients into the hands of doctors who are keen to test new treatments. Patients do not always know what they are getting into. Therefore, a system was created that paired a "patient advocate" with the first volunteer to receive an implanted mechanical heart.

1. 医療実験（　　　　　）（　　　　　）
2. 弱い（　　　　　　　　　　　　　）
3. 埋め込み式の（　　　　　　　　　）
4. 人工心臓（　　　　　）（　　　　　）
5. 患者代弁人（　　　　　）（　　　　　）

Listening 34

CD を聴いて、写真の説明として適切なものを a ～ d から選びましょう。

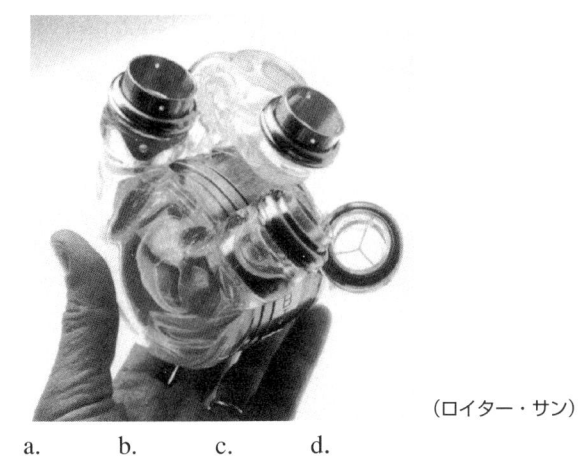

（ロイター・サン）

a.　　b.　　c.　　d.

Mechanical heart recipient paired with advocate

The first testing of the artificial heart is daring. Only patients who are very sick will be selected, and they will have to have their heart removed and an electrically powered device is implanted. The mechanical heart, made by Massachusetts-based ABIOMED Inc., has worked quite well in young cows, but only now has the first test in a human volunteer begun.

An independent patient advocacy council was, therefore, established for the first five heart implant experiments. Patient advocates have been used before, but usually as part of a hospital or research team's staff, not as wholly independent outsiders. Under this new independent advocacy system, the patient advocates are paid expenses and fees from a trust fund.

Patients in experiments like the heart trial risk extreme discomfort because they are already so sick and death is likely. The goal of this advocacy system is to make sure patients understand the hazards, the potential benefits, the alternatives, and what it will mean to be the subject in a daring and dangerous experiment.

The first test of the implanted heart was on a man in his late 50s. Doctors said the patient was a very sick man when he arrived at Jewish Hospital, not expected to live beyond 30 days because of congestive heart failure. He was reported doing better than expected in the first week after surgery. If he manages to survive 60 days or even longer, this first test will be considered a success.

The people at ABIOMED hope the artificial heart will be widely used to save lives. The heart and its battery-pack power system are designed for use at home, so it can readily be plugged into an electric outlet to recharge when the batteries run down. Patients would carry spare charged batteries when away from home. This pioneering test of the device is also the first test of the new patient advocacy system.

(*Newsday.com*, July 17, 2001)
©2001 Newsday, Inc. Reprinted with permission,

1. 世界初の人工心臓移植手術について、ここで述べられている内容と合わないものを選びましょう。

a. 非常に重症の患者だけが受けることができる。
b. 患者自身の心臓は取り除かれる。
c. 人工心臓は電動である。
d. その人工心臓は、これまでサルで試されてきた。

2. 患者の代弁人制度について、ここで述べられている内容と合わないものを選びましょう。

a. 世界初の人工心臓移植実験のために、新たに独立した協議会が組織された。
b. 人工心臓移植手術の前は、代弁人はまったく利用されていなかった。
c. これまでの代弁人は、病院や研究スタッフの一員であった。
d. 新たな独立代弁人制度では、代弁人の報酬は信託基金から支払われる。

3. 患者代弁人の目的として、ここで述べられている内容と合わないものを選びましょう。

a. 患者が不安から逃れるには臨床試験を受ける以外に手段がないことを理解させる。
b. 臨床試験に伴う危険性を患者に理解させる。
c. 臨床試験以外に選択できる方法について、患者に理解させる。
d. 大胆で危険性の高い臨床試験の被験者になることの意味を、患者に理解させる。

4. 世界初の人工心臓移植実験を受けた患者について、ここで述べられている内容と合わないものを選びましょう。

a. 来院した時点で、30日以上は生きられないと予想されていた。
b. 来院した時点で、うっ血性の心不全のためにすでに容態が悪かった。
c. 手術後1週間は予想外に調子がよかった。
d. 移植実験が成功したと言えるために、手術後60日以上生き続けたいと自ら語った。

5. アビオメド社の開発した人工心臓について、ここで述べられている内容と合うものを選びましょう。

a. この人工心臓は、病院で使用するように設計されている。
b. この人工心臓のプラグは、常にコンセントに差し込まれている必要がある。
c. この人工心臓の電源用の電池は充電式である。
d. この人工心臓を移植された患者は外出できない。

Grammar

下線部a〜cの中で語法が誤っているものを選び、訂正しましょう。

1. The patient underwent surgeries to stop _a<u>bleed</u> from stitches and to _b<u>remove</u> fluid _c<u>accumulating</u> near his new heart.

    [   ] → _____

2. An ethicist _a<u>was</u> recruited by ABIOMED specifically to _b<u>making</u> sure there _c<u>were</u> no ethical barriers to running the experiments.

    [   ] → _____

Vocabulary

A. 下線部に入る適切な語をa〜cから選びましょう。

1. The advocate's role includes ensuring that a patient is not subjected to inappropriate _____ from doctors.
    a. price   b. pressure   c. presents

2. In the desperate search for help, patients tend to minimize the _____ , while magnifying the hope.
    a. hazards   b. happiness   c. heart

3. Because researchers are enthusiastic about the possibilities of their new idea, they may unconsciously _____ what they have got.
    a. overtake   b. sell   c. oversell

B. この Unit のトピックに関わる１〜７の基本語句について、対応する英語を枠内から選んで記入しましょう。

1. 人工心臓　　　（　　　　　　）
2. 電動の　　　　（　　　　　　）
3. 心不全　　　　（　　　　　　）
4. 移植する　　　（　　　　　　）
5. 電池　　　　　（　　　　　　）
6. 装置　　　　　（　　　　　　）
7. 被験者　　　　（　　　　　　）

```
artificial heart
battery
device
electrically powered
heart failure
implant
subject
```

Unit 18 献血したことありますか？

Orientation

枠内の下線部 1～5 は英語で何というでしょうか。下記の英文を参考にして、対応する語句を書き出しましょう。

> 1990年代、アメリカ政府はAIDSウイルスから輸血用の₁血液供給を₂守るために、FDAが監督するいくつかの₃規定を設けました。その結果、血液₄供給源として支障なく献血できる人の数は減少してしまいました。それにもかかわらず、政府は最近、狂牛病の感染を防ぐ目的で、新たな規定を₅制定しようとしています。

The U.S. government is going to enact regulations aimed at safeguarding the nation's blood supply from mad cow disease. The new rules will come on top of the federal regulations issued in the last decade that would keep the AIDS virus out of the blood supply. Yet, these old rules already have reduced the nation's normal donor pool.

1. 血液供給（　　　　）（　　　　）　4. 供給源（　　　　）（　　　　）

2. 守る（　　　　　　　　　）　5. 制定する（　　　　　　　　　）

3. 規定（　　　　　　　　　）

Listening 36

CDを聴いて、イラストの説明として適切なものをa～dから選びましょう。

a.　　b.　　c.　　d.

(KINKO TAMAMAKI)

Blood supply could dry up

In the cases of most hospitalizations or other emergencies, the blood needed to keep people alive must come from another human being. Yet, the latest data show that just five percent of Americans healthy enough to donate blood do so. And that percentage is even lower in the biggest cities.

For years, this has added up to serious blood shortages at most city hospitals, generally during the year-end holidays and at mid-summer. If the Food and Drug Administration enacted donation restrictions prompted by mad cow disease, those shortages eventually could turn into one yearlong crisis. And yet, the need for blood has risen in hospitals, trauma centers, and clinics.

Under the new FDA plan, blood banks will have to bar donors who have spent three or more cumulative months in Britain from 1980 through 1996, spent five or more cumulative years in France from 1980 to the present, or received a blood transfusion in Britain since 1980. The FDA estimates that the new rules will eliminate five percent of current blood donors.

Sixty or 70 years ago, the problems about the roundup of donors were few. Americans in wartime, and as recently as the 1950s, would jump at an emergency appeal for blood. But society has changed. As a result, patients in hospitals frequently must put off elective surgery because of the lack of blood on hand.

More people are working longer hours, even though donating blood requires no more than 40 or 50 minutes. Moreover, since the early 1980s, when news of AIDS exploded across the country, fewer and fewer Americans have turned out for blood drives. Many people hear the word "needle" and react negatively without realizing that HIV has never been contracted by donating blood.

(*Chicago Tribune*, September 8, 2001)

1 輸血用血液に関するアメリカの現状として、ここで述べられている内容と合うものを選びましょう。
a. 入院時や緊急時の輸血用血液は、血縁者以外から提供を受けることになっている。
b. 最新のデータでは、献血に支障のない健康な人は全人口の5％ほどにすぎない。
c. 最新のデータでは、献血した経験がある人は全人口の5％ほどにすぎない。
d. 人口に対する献血経験者の割合は、大都市の方がその他の地方よりも少ない。

2 血液提供に関するFDAの新たな規制が実施された場合、どんな事態が起こると予想されているでしょうか。
a. 年末や盛夏の時期の輸血用血液不足が解消される。
b. 狂牛病の影響によって、毎年規制を強化する必要が生じる。
c. 都市部での血液供給が年間を通して不足する。
d. 病院や医療センター・診療所などの患者が増える。

3 FDAの新たな規制実施後でも献血に支障がないと思われる人を選びましょう。
a. イギリスでの滞在が、1980年から1996年までに合わせて3ヶ月以上の人
b. フランスでの滞在が、1980年から現在までに合わせて5年以上の人
c. 1980年以降、イギリス滞在中に輸血を受けた経験のある人
d. 現時点における血液提供者のうち、95％の人

4 ここで述べられている内容と合うものを選びましょう。
a. 今から60～70年前も、血液提供者はなかなか集まらなかった。
b. 1950年代以降、アメリカ人は献血を求める緊急の呼びかけに対して快く応じなくなった。
c. 社会の変化とともに、手術を必要とする患者の数は激減している。
d. 最近、入院患者に対して緊急を要しない手術はしばしば延期されるようになった。

5 現代のアメリカ人が献血をしなくなっている理由として、ここで述べられている内容と合うものを選びましょう。
a. 労働時間が長くなり、わずか1時間足らずの献血に割く時間さえ持てない。
b. 1980年代初頭のAIDS騒動以降、献血を呼びかけるキャンペーンがだんだん減ってきている。
c. 献血に使われる注射針の痛みをいやがる人が増えている。
d. 献血によってHIVに感染した事例がニュースで流れた。

Grammar

下線部a～cの中で語法が誤っているものを選び、訂正しましょう。

1. There is _a<u>no evidence</u> _b<u>which</u> mad cow disease ever has _c<u>been transmitted</u> through blood transfusions.

    [　] → _____

2. A teenager said, "My mother _a<u>was</u> in the hospital and, before she _b<u>dies</u> of breast cancer, I saw how important _c<u>it was</u> to donate blood."

    [　] → _____

Vocabulary

A. 下線部に入る適切な語をa～cから選びましょう。

1. The act of donating has been proved in research laboratories to _____ the risks of heart attacks and cancer.
    a. reduce   b. spend   c. run

2. The FDA will bar donors who spent a _____ five years or more anywhere in Europe since 1980.
    a. complex   b. concrete   c. cumulative

3. For young people, the best chance to feel the need for blood _____ may be an injury or death in their family.
    a. cancers   b. donations   c. shortages

B. この Unit のトピックに関わる１～７の基本語句について、対応する英語を枠内から選んで記入しましょう。

1. 入院　　　　　　　(　　　　　　　)
2. 緊急事態　　　　　(　　　　　　　)
3. 提供する　　　　　(　　　　　　　)
4. 献血キャンペーン　(　　　　　　　)
5. 血液不足　　　　　(　　　　　　　)
6. 感染する　　　　　(　　　　　　　)
7. 輸血　　　　　　　(　　　　　　　)

```
donate
blood transfusion
emergency
blood shortage
hospitalization
contract
blood drive
```

Unit 19 今、産むべきか産まざるべきか

Orientation

枠内の下線部 1 ～ 5 は英語で何というでしょうか。下記の英文を参考にして、対応する語句を書き出しましょう。

> 女性の社会進出が目覚しい中、高齢₁出産を目指す女性が増えつつあります。20数年前の₂試験管ベビー₃誕生以降、₄体外受精(IVF)など、さまざまな₅不妊治療技術も進歩を遂げつつあり、その風潮を助長しているようです。しかし、女性の卵子が老化するにつれ、受胎し出産に至る可能性はどんどん低下するという生物学的事実に変りはないのです。

The media are filled with miraculous stories of women over 40 becoming mothers. And headlines touting the latest technological advances such as in vitro fertilization since test-tube baby's birth make the childbearing by matured women all sound so easy. But the truth is it's not. We should understand the severity of aging as a risk factor for infertility.

1. 出産（　　　　　　　　）
2. 試験管ベビー（　　　　）（　　　　）
3. 誕生（　　　　　　　　　　）
4. 体外受精（　　　）（　　　）（　　　）
5. 不妊（　　　　　　　　　　）

Listening 38

CD を聴いて、イラストの説明として適切なものを a ～ d から選びましょう。

a.　　b.　　c.　　d.

(KINKO TAMAMAKI)

Should you have your baby now?

Women are delaying childbearing as never before. In America, there is a general assumption that, if you can't have children, you go through in vitro fertilization (IVF) and get them. But in reality, only about 2 percent of all babies are born to women over 40 every year. The live birthrate per IVF treatment is 20 to 25 percent for women under 28; for those over 40, it's 5 percent or less.

A woman is born with a finite number of eggs, which gradually get ovulated or die off as she ages. And older eggs have a harder time making it through the fertilization process. By 30, fertility rates begin to slowly decline. By 43, older eggs are far more likely to develop chromosomal abnormalities. Miscarriage soars as women age — from about 15 percent in women 25 to 30, to about 40 percent in women over 40.

Technology has worked wonders. Researchers can now not only mix egg and sperm in a petri dish, but can genetically test embryos for certain abnormalities, then weed them out before implantation. In treating male infertility, a single, sluggish sperm can be hunted down, then injected directly into an egg. And now donor eggs can be sucked out of one woman's ovaries and transferred to another's.

And now scientists have been looking for new ways to attack the most frustrating problem in infertility today: the older woman's egg. German doctor Hans van der Ven has successfully implanted eggs that had been frozen for nine years. Already, researchers have experimented with a procedure called "nuclear transfer," in which they suck the nucleus out of an older woman's egg, and then transfer it into a cytoplasm of a younger egg.

These technologies are after all experimental and may never be available to humans. Some variations of nuclear transfer have already run into a major stumbling block because the experiments involve a process that uses some of the same steps involved in cloning. And the technology that does exist — IVF — is financially, physically and emotionally draining. What's more, success rates decline significantly as women age: we haven't seen any real improvements in treating women over 40. You can't change biology.

(*Newsweek*, August 27, 2001)

1 ここで述べられている内容と合うものを選びましょう。
a. 出産を遅らせたいと望む若い女性が増えてきている。
b. アメリカの女性の多くが、赤ちゃんが生まれなければ、体外受精で産めばよいと考えている。
c. 毎年、40歳以上の女性のうち2パーセントしか赤ちゃんを授からない。
d. 女性は年齢が高くなるほど、体外受精で赤ちゃんを産みやすくなる。

2 ここで述べられている内容と合わないものを選びましょう。
a. 女性は生まれた時から、決まった数の卵子をもっていて徐々に排卵される。
b. 卵子は年を重ねるごとに成熟して受精しやすくなっていく。
c. 女性が40歳を超えると、卵子に遺伝子異常が起こる確率が高くなる。
d. 40歳を超えて妊娠した女性の約4割が流産している。

3 研究者たちが行っている活動と合わないものを選びましょう。
a. ペトリ皿の上で卵子と精子を混合させる。
b. 異常な遺伝子を持つ胚を見つけ出し、取り除く。
c. 機能の低下した精子を見つけて殺す。
d. 卵子提供者の卵子を卵巣から吸い出し、別の女性の卵巣に移す。

4 「卵子の老化」の問題に対処するために行われているものを選びましょう。
a. アメリカの医師が、9年間冷凍保存していた卵子の移植に成功した。
b. 老化した卵子を吸い出して殺していく。
c. 年取った女性の卵子の核を吸い出して、若い女性の卵子の細胞質（cytoplasm）の中に入れる。
d. 若い女性の卵子を冷凍しておき、卵子バンクに登録する。

5 ここで述べられている内容と合わないものを選びましょう。
a. 古い卵子の問題を解決するための技術は、全てまだ実験段階にある。
b. 古い卵子の「核移植」はクローニングと同じ手順を含むため、障害にぶつかっている。
c. 「体外受精」は、経済的・肉体的・感情的にも患者を消耗させるものである。
d. 40歳以上の女性の不妊治療の成功率は目覚しく上がっている。

Grammar

下線部a～cの中で語法が誤っているものを選び、訂正しましょう。

1. Among healthy couples _ain their mid-20s who _bis not using birth control, about one in four will get pregnant each _cmonth.

    [ ] → _____

2. In the future some kind of _afreezing technique could _bbe available for healthy young women who just _cwants to wait.

    [ ] → _____

Vocabulary

A. 下線部に入る適切な語をa～cから選びましょう。

1. The greatest risk is pushing _____ to the late 30s and 40s.
    a. childbearing   b. child-caring   c. childhood

2. As women _____, their eggs become more susceptible to genetic errors.
    a. are born   b. get younger   c. age

3. The rate of first _____ for women in their 30s and 40s has surged all over the world.
    a. birthdays   b. births   c. fertility

B. このUnitのトピックに関わる１～７の基本語句について、対応する英語を枠内から選んで記入しましょう。

1. 遅らせる   (   )
2. 細胞核の   (   )
3. 流産   (   )
4. 移植   (   )
5. 卵巣   (   )
6. 排卵する   (   )
7. 出生率   (   )

> birthrate
> implantation
> nuclear
> miscarriage
> delay
> ovary
> ovulate

Unit 20 進化の果ては？

Orientation

枠内の下線部 1 ～ 5 は英語で何というでしょうか。下記の英文を参考にして、対応する語句を書き出しましょう。

地球上の様々な生物が、以前よりも₁進化の速度を速めているようです。その₂推進力と考えられているのは、急激に進歩した人類の技術です。たとえば、抗生物質が導入されたとたんにバクテリアが₃抵抗力を強める事例や、害虫の₄種が₅殺虫剤への耐性を高めるよう進化を遂げることが報告されています。もっとも、文明の進展は、さらに危険な「進化」を生んでいるようです。

Humans are now the dominant driving force behind evolution, because of the massive impact of technology. This is most clearly seen in the speed of the evolution of bacterial resistance to antibiotics. No sooner are new antibiotics used than a new strain of resistant disease turns up. It is the same with insecticides and pest species. Yet, scientists say that the danger goes further than that.

1. 進化（　　　　　　　　　）　4. 種（　　　　　　　　　）

2. 推進力（　　　　　）（　　　　　）　5. 殺虫剤（　　　　　　　　　）

3. 抵抗力（　　　　　　　　　）

Listening 🄲🄳 40

CD を聴いて、イラストの説明として適切なものを a ～ d から選びましょう。

a.　　b.　　c.　　d.

(KINKO TAMAMAKI)

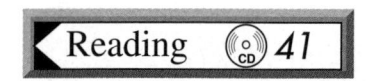

Evolution : Who's responsible?

The human impact on earth has been well-documented: There's climate change, environmental destruction and pollution. Today, Stephen Palumbi, an American evolutionary biologist, says that humans are driving another change that may have consequences that are just as damaging: Evolution in other species is speeding up, and we are to blame.

Penicillin was first widely used in 1943. By 1946, however, resistance was reported. The Swiss scientist Paul Muller discovered in 1939 that DDT killed insects. By the time he was awarded the Nobel Prize in 1948 for his research, houseflies had already evolved resistance. Bacteria can evolve resistance even faster than insects. Viruses are faster still.

"I hope that people begin to realize the power of rapid evolution — and, instead of waiting for it to happen, begin taking actions ahead of time. Overuse of antibiotics has been one of the main problems," says Palumbi. So he recommends withholding the most powerful new drugs, and thus preventing bacteria from developing resistance.

Meanwhile, the physicist Stephen Hawking says that there is a real danger that computer intelligence will surpass that of humans — with the worrying implication that computer intelligence will take over the world. He advises that humans increase the rate of our own evolution by genetic manipulation so as to improve our health and intelligence.

Decrease the speed of evolution of other organisms, but increase that of humans. Should we follow this road? Palumbi says, "Hawking's solution creates even more problems. Increasing the complexity of human DNA is not necessary — the current genome is 10 times larger than needed — nor ethical. However, I agree that machine evolution is a real problem for the future."

(By Rowan Hooper, *The Japan Times*, September 6, 2001)

1 人間の活動が地球に与えている悪影響として、ここで述べられていないものを選びましょう。

a. 気象の変化
b. 環境の破壊
c. 人口爆発による食糧不足
d. 生物の進化する速度が速くなっていること

2 この段落で強調されていることを選びましょう。

a. ペニシリンの効果が予想よりも強かったこと
b. ノーベル賞の価値が高いこと
c. バクテリアの抵抗力がかなり強いこと
d. 生物の進化する速度がかなり速いこと

3 生物の急速な進化を抑えるために、Palumbi がここで提案している具体策を選びましょう。

a. 目に見える進化が起こるのを待つこと
b. 抗生物質を多量に使用すること
c. 強力な効果を持つ新薬の使用を避けること
d. バクテリアの抵抗力をさらに高めること

4 Hawking が「現実の危険性」として挙げていることを選びましょう。

a. コンピュータの知能が人間を進化させること
b. コンピュータの知能が世界を支配すること
c. 人間が自らの進化の速度を上げること
d. 人間が遺伝子操作によって知能を高めること

5 Palumbi と Hawking の見解が一致している点を選びましょう。

a. Hawking の提案が問題を解決するということ
b. 人間の遺伝子構造を複雑にする必要があること
c. 人間の遺伝子情報は必要以上に多いこと
d. 機械の進化が人間の将来にとって大問題であること

Grammar

下線部a~cの中で語法が誤っているものを選び、訂正しましょう。

1. _aIncreasing the rate of human evolution by genetic _bengineer is the only way for us to stay _cahead of artificial intelligence.

    [　] → _____

2. _aDuring this century, we will discover _bhow to modify complex characteristics _csame as intelligence.

    [　] → _____

Vocabulary

A. 下線部に入る適切な語をa~cから選びましょう。

1. Human ecological impact can greatly _____ evolutionary change in the species on the earth.
    a. reduce   b. accelerate   c. select

2. Recently, because fish have to pass through fishing _____, their bodies have been found to grow more slowly and thinner.
    a. nets   b. boats   c. shops

3. We may have to manipulate our genes if we want biological systems to remain _____ to electronic ones.
    a. inferior   b. same   c. superior

B. このUnitのトピックに関わる1~7の基本語句について、対応する英語を枠内から選んで記入しましょう。

1. 環境破壊　　（　　　　　　）
2. 人工知能　　（　　　　　　）
3. 乱用　　　　（　　　　　　）
4. ゲノム　　　（　　　　　　）
5. 遺伝子操作　（　　　　　　）
6. 進化する　　（　　　　　　）
7. 倫理的な　　（　　　　　　）

```
ethical
overuse
genetic manipulation
environmental destruction
genome
artificial intelligence
evolve
```

Curing the Future
―Current Topics of Health―
健康を科学する

2003年1月20日　初版　発行
2024年3月15日　第15刷　発行

著　者　椋平 淳・深山 晶子・川越 栄子
　　　　玉巻 欣子・早瀬 淳一・福田 慎司
発行者　佐野 英一郎
発行所　株式会社 成美堂
　　　　〒101-0052　東京都千代田区神田小川町3-22
　　　　TEL 03-3291-2261　FAX 03-3293-5490
　　　　https://www.seibido.co.jp

印刷・製本　　（株）加藤文明社
表紙デザイン　Atelier Z

ISBN 978-4-7919-4067-7　　　　Printed in Japan

・落丁・乱丁本はお取り替えします。
・本書の無断複写は、著作権上の例外を除き著作権侵害となります。